BEST LOVED RECIPES

BEST LOVED RECIPES

CELEBRATING
75 YEARS
OF GREAT BAKING

LAND O' LAKES
PUBLISHER
Lydia Botham
EDITOR
Mary Sue Peterson
COORDINATING FOOD EDITOR
Cindy Manwarren
SENIOR PROJECT COORDINATOR
Carolyn Patten

TIME-LIFE CUSTOM PUBLISHING
VICE PRESIDENT AND PUBLISHER
Terry Newell
DIRECTOR OF SALES
Neil Levin
DIRECTOR OF MARKETING
Rebecca C. Wheeler
SENIOR ACCOUNT EXECUTIVE
Wendy Blythe
PROGRAM MANAGER
Trish Palini
PROJECT MANAGER
Sally Collins
PRODUCTION MANAGER
Carolyn Mills Bounds
QUALITY ASSURANCE MANAGER
Jim King

Land O' Lakes BEST LOVED RECIPES
was designed by Susan K. White.

First printing
Printed in U.S.A.

TIME-LIFE is a trademark of
Time Warner Inc. U.S.A.

Recipes developed and tested by the
Land O' Lakes Test Kitchens.

LIBRARY OF CONGRESS CATALOGING-IN-PUBLICATION DATA

Best-loved recipes
p. cm.
Includes index.
Cover title: Land O' Lakes best loved recipes. ISBN 0-7835-4860-5
1. Desserts. 2. Name brand products.
I. Land O' Lakes, Inc. II. Title:
Land O' Lakes best loved recipes
TX773.B4867 1996
641.8'65—dc20   96-25442
                              CIP

Books produced by Time-Life Custom Publishing are available at special bulk discount for promotional and premium use. Call 1-800-323-5255.

CONTENTS

THE LAND O'LAKES STORY

A GOLDEN REWARD was offered to the person who could come up with the perfect name. In 1924 the Minnesota Cooperative Creameries Association had been marketing outstanding dairy products for three years, and now it needed a brand name that would stand out in the minds of homemakers, and indicate the pride and quality that went into their products. Inspired by the warm yellow hue of their butter, the Association offered $200 in gold as first prize in the contest. Out of 100,000 entries, Ida Foss and George Swift each received the golden prize for separately submitting the winning name: Land O'Lakes.

Since that day, Land O'Lakes has been a leader in providing the freshest and most delicious dairy products nationwide. And they have been outstanding in the field of agricultural research and development too, offering dairymen and other farmers new feeds and new techniques to increase production and ensure superior quality.

For Minnesota dairymen of the early 1920s, one discovery led to a revolutionary change in butter production. Supported by research from the U.S. Department of Agriculture, John Brandt, a dairy farmer from Litchfield, and a leader in Minnesota's cooperative creamery movement, urged creameries to make butter from fresh, sweet cream instead of sour cream as was then the practice. The butter made from sour cream was very uneven in quality, leading

consumers to complain of butter that "smelt bad, tasted worse and did not keep at all." By switching to sweet cream, the butter quality could be assured, even as it was shipped under refrigeration from state to state.

America loved the change. The new sweet cream butter from Land O' Lakes replaced the traditional 50-pound tubs from which grocers had hand-packed butter upon the customer's request. Butter was also packaged in one-pound rolls double-wrapped in waxed paper, or in the four quarter-pound sticks we are familiar with today. Land O' Lakes was even able to boast that its new sweet cream butter was favored by President Calvin Coolidge, who placed a stand-

ing order for Land O' Lakes butter on the presidential yacht!

As the years sped by new products were added to the roster. By the 1930s, the cooperative dairies of Land O' Lakes were producing and marketing butter, milk, eggs, turkey, cheese, ice cream, salad dressing and even furniture wax and paint. During World War II, stateside rationing cut consumer butter purchases in half, but sales were made up by government requisitions of powdered milk for GIs overseas.

Once the war was over, returning soldiers and their families took part in the nation's growing prosperity, and so did Land O' Lakes. The company continued to grow and de-

velop diverse businesses and fleets of Land O' Lakes trucks delivered fresh dairy products to the new supermarkets that were popping up across the country. But for America's cooks, one special feature of Land O' Lakes was—and continues to be—very much appreciated: its test kitchens.

Since the 1930s, the Land O' Lakes Test Kitchens have been busy developing recipes to showcase their butter and other dairy products. Today, through their Land O' Lakes® Recipe Collections, published six times a year, Land O' Lakes home economists show home cooks how to prepare tasty new main dishes and special treats for busy families. Additional support comes from the Land O' Lakes Consumer Affairs division. In operation since the 1970s, Consumer Affairs responds to 100,000 customer concerns and inquiries annually through its toll-free phone line. During the busy holiday season, tips from professional home economists on the Holiday Bakeline help home cooks avoid kitchen disasters.

As America's tastes have changed, Land O'Lakes has responded with more and more new products including No•Fat and Light Sour Cream, Light Butter and American Cheese that is a nationwide favorite at supermarket deli counters. All of these products are made to the same exacting standards of quality established 75 years ago, and it is this high quality of Land O' Lakes products that home cooks have come to depend on over the years.

The recipes in this book represent over 70 all-time favorites from the Land O' Lakes Test Kitchens. There are new versions of traditional favorites, such as scones enlivened with dill and shredded Land O' Lakes® Cheddar (page 47). Or try an imaginative creation that brings together ingredients in flavorful new combinations: The Apple Crisp Cake on page 69, for example, marries a rich apple cake with a crunchy sweet topping usually found on apple crisp. You will also find tried-and-true recipes for Favorite Butter Cookies (page 26), Old-World Raspberry Bars (page 18), and Lemon Poppy Seed Pound Cake (page 71). And for recipes that call for sour cream, such as Cranberry Sour Cream Crumble (page 51) or Chocolate Brownie Almond Bundt Cake (page 62), Land O' Lakes lets you choose from three varieties: Regular, Light or No•Fat Sour Cream.

So gather your family and friends around the dinner table and reward them with something special, something you've made with your heart and hands—and with a little help from the heartland.

THE FAMILIES OF
LAND O' LAKES

COOKIES

ho can resist a freshly baked cookie? Whether it is a gooey lemon square, a crisp sugar cookie or a classic chocolate chip, these mouth-watering delights are proven crowd pleasers. Use LAND O LAKES® Butter for golden cookies with just the right texture!

Glazed Apple Pie Bars

PREPARATION TIME: 1 hour
BAKING TIME: 45 minutes

YIELD: 36 bars

CRUST

2½ cups all-purpose flour
1   teaspoon salt
1   cup LAND O LAKES® Butter, chilled
1   egg, separated, yolk beaten with enough milk to equal ⅔ cup, <u>reserve white</u>

FILLING

1   cup crushed cornflakes
8 to 10 medium (8 cups) tart cooking apples, peeled, sliced
1   cup sugar
1½ teaspoons cinnamon
½   teaspoon ground nutmeg

1   reserved egg white
2   tablespoons sugar
½   teaspoon cinnamon

GLAZE

1   cup powdered sugar
½   teaspoon vanilla
1 to 2 tablespoons milk

❖ Heat oven to 350°. In medium bowl combine flour and salt; cut in butter until crumbly. With fork, stir in egg yolk and milk until dough forms a ball; divide in half. On lightly floured surface roll <u>one half</u> of dough into 15x10-inch rectangle; place on bottom of 15x10x1-inch jelly roll pan. Sprinkle with cornflakes; top with apples.

❖ In small bowl combine 1 cup sugar, 1½ teaspoons cinnamon and nutmeg. Sprinkle over apples. Roll remaining half of dough into 15½x10½-inch rectangle; place over apples.

❖ In small bowl beat egg white with fork until foamy; brush over top crust. In small bowl stir together 2 tablespoons sugar and ½ teaspoon cinnamon; sprinkle over crust. Bake for 45 to 60 minutes or until lightly browned.

❖ In small bowl stir together powdered sugar, vanilla and enough milk for desired glazing consistency. Drizzle over warm bars.

NUTRITION FACTS (1 BAR)			
Calories	130	Fat	5g
Protein	1g	Cholesterol	20mg
Carbohydrate	20g	Sodium	120mg

CHOCOLATE PIXIES

PREPARATION TIME: 45 minutes
CHILLING TIME: 2 hours   BAKING TIME: 12 minutes

YIELD: 4 dozen cookies

¼ cup LAND O LAKES® Butter

4 (1-ounce) squares unsweetened baking chocolate

2 cups all-purpose flour

2 cups sugar

4 eggs

2 teaspoons baking powder

½ teaspoon salt

½ cup chopped walnuts or pecans

Powdered sugar

❖ In 1-quart saucepan melt butter and chocolate over low heat (8 to 10 minutes); cool.

❖ In large mixer bowl combine melted chocolate mixture, 1 cup flour and all remaining ingredients except nuts and powdered sugar. Beat at medium speed, scraping bowl often, until well mixed (2 to 3 minutes). By hand, stir in remaining flour and nuts. Cover; refrigerate at least 2 hours.

❖ Heat oven to 300°. Shape rounded teaspoonfuls of dough into 1-inch balls; roll in powdered sugar. Place 2 inches apart on greased cookie sheets. Bake for 12 to 15 minutes or until firm to the touch.

NUTRITION FACTS		
(1 COOKIE)		
Calories	90	Fat	3g
Protein	2g	Cholesterol	20mg
Carbohydrate	13g	Sodium	50mg

English Toffee Bars

PREPARATION TIME: 30 minutes
BAKING TIME: 40 minutes

YIELD: 48 bars

1 cup sugar
1 cup LAND O LAKES® Butter, softened
1 egg, separated
1¾ cups all-purpose flour
1 teaspoon cinnamon
1 cup chopped pecans

1 cup milk or semi-sweet real chocolate chips

❖ Heat oven to 275°. In small mixer bowl combine sugar and butter. Beat at medium speed, scraping bowl often, until creamy. Add egg yolk; continue beating until well mixed. Reduce speed to low. Beat, gradually adding flour and cinnamon, until well mixed. Press evenly on bottom of 15x10x1-inch jelly roll pan.

❖ In small bowl, with fork, beat egg white; brush over top of dough. Sprinkle with pecans; pat lightly into dough. Bake for 40 to 50 minutes or until edges are lightly browned.

❖ Sprinkle with chocolate chips; let stand 3 minutes. With knife, swirl chips slightly. Cut while warm into squares, triangles or diamonds. Cool completely.

N U T R I T I O N		F A C T S	
(1 BAR)			
Calories	100	Fat	7g
Protein	1g	Cholesterol	15mg
Carbohydrate	10g	Sodium	45mg

Chunky Peanut Cookies

PREPARATION TIME: 40 minutes
BAKING TIME: 8 minutes

YIELD: 4 dozen cookies

1¾ cups all-purpose flour
½ cup firmly packed brown sugar
½ cup sugar
½ cup LAND O LAKES® Butter, softened
2 eggs
1 teaspoon salt
½ teaspoon baking soda
½ teaspoon vanilla
2 cups salted cocktail peanuts

❖ Heat oven to 350°. In large mixer bowl combine all ingredients except peanuts. Beat at low speed, scraping bowl often, until well mixed (2 to 3 minutes). By hand, stir in peanuts.

❖ Drop dough by rounded teaspoonfuls 2 inches apart onto greased cookie sheets. Bake for 8 to 12 minutes or until lightly browned.

N U T R I T I O N		F A C T S	
(1 COOKIE)			
Calories	90	Fat	6g
Protein	2g	Cholesterol	15mg
Carbohydrate	9g	Sodium	140mg

Caramel n' Chocolate Pecan Bars

PREPARATION TIME: 30 minutes
BAKING TIME: 18 minutes

YIELD: 36 bars

CRUST

2 cups all-purpose flour
1 cup firmly packed brown sugar
½ cup LAND O LAKES® Butter, softened
1 cup pecan halves

CARAMEL LAYER

⅔ cup LAND O LAKES® Butter
½ cup firmly packed brown sugar

1 (6-ounce) package (1 cup) semi-sweet real chocolate chips

❖ Heat oven to 350°. In large mixer bowl combine all crust ingredients except pecans. Beat at medium speed, scraping bowl often, until well mixed and particles are fine (2 to 3 minutes). Press on bottom of 13x9-inch baking pan. Sprinkle pecans evenly over unbaked crust.

❖ In 1-quart saucepan combine ⅔ cup butter and ½ cup brown sugar. Cook over medium heat, stirring constantly, until mixture comes to a full boil. Boil, stirring constantly, until candy thermometer reaches 242°F or small amount of mixture dropped into ice water forms a firm ball (about 1 minute). Pour evenly over pecans and crust.

❖ Bake for 18 to 22 minutes or until entire caramel layer is bubbly. Remove from oven. Sprinkle with chocolate chips; let stand 2 to 3 minutes. With knife, swirl chips leaving some whole for marbled effect. Cool completely; cut into bars.

NUTRITION FACTS			
(1 BAR)			
Calories	160	Fat	10g
Protein	1g	Cholesterol	15mg
Carbohydrate	18g	Sodium	70mg

Melt-in-Your-Mouth Spritz

PREPARATION TIME: 1 hour
BAKING TIME: 6 minutes

YIELD: 5 dozen cookies

⅔ cup sugar
1 cup LAND O LAKES® Butter, softened
1 egg
½ teaspoon salt
2 teaspoons vanilla
2¼ cups all-purpose flour

❖ Heat oven to 400°. In large mixer bowl combine all ingredients <u>except</u> flour. Beat at medium speed, scraping bowl often, until creamy (2 to 3 minutes).

❖ Reduce speed to low; add flour. Beat, scraping bowl often, until well mixed (2 to 3 minutes). If desired, add ingredients from one of the following variations. If dough is too soft, cover; refrigerate until firm enough to form cookies (30 to 45 minutes).

❖ Place dough in cookie press; form desired shapes 1 inch apart on cookie sheets. Bake for 6 to 8 minutes or until edges are lightly browned.

VARIATIONS

❖ Chocolate Flecked Spritz: To dough add ¼ cup coarsely grated semisweet chocolate.

❖ Chocolate Mint Spritz: To dough add ¼ teaspoon mint extract. Immediately after removing cookies from oven place 1 chocolate candy kiss on each cookie.

❖ Eggnog Spritz: To dough add 1 teaspoon ground nutmeg. Glaze: In small bowl stir together 1 cup powdered sugar, ¼ cup LAND O LAKES® Butter, softened, 2 tablespoons water and ¼ teaspoon rum extract until smooth; drizzle over warm cookies.

❖ Spiced Spritz: To dough add 1 teaspoon cinnamon, 1 teaspoon ground nutmeg, ½ teaspoon ground allspice and ¼ teaspoon ground cloves. Glaze: In small bowl stir together 1 cup powdered sugar, 2 tablespoons milk and ½ teaspoon vanilla until smooth; drizzle over warm cookies.

NUTRITION FACTS (1 COOKIE)			
Calories	50	Fat	3g
Protein	1g	Cholesterol	10mg
Carbohydrate	6g	Sodium	50mg

Simply Fudgy Saucepan Brownies

PREPARATION TIME: 15 minutes   BAKING TIME: 25 minutes
COOLING TIME: 30 minutes

YIELD: 16 brownies

BROWNIES

½ cup LAND O LAKES® Butter
2 (1-ounce) squares unsweetened baking chocolate
1 cup sugar
¾ cup all-purpose flour
2 eggs

FROSTING

¼ cup LAND O LAKES® Butter
3 tablespoons milk
1 (1-ounce) square unsweetened baking chocolate
2½ cups powdered sugar
½ teaspoon vanilla

❖ Heat oven to 350°. In 2-quart saucepan combine ½ cup butter and 2 squares chocolate. Cook over medium heat, stirring constantly, until melted (3 to 5 minutes). Stir in all remaining brownie ingredients until well mixed.

❖ Spread into greased 9-inch square baking pan. Bake for 25 to 30 minutes or until brownies begin to pull away from sides of pan.

❖ In same saucepan combine butter, milk and chocolate; bring to a full boil. Remove from heat. Add powdered sugar; beat until smooth. Stir in vanilla. Frost brownies while warm. Cool; cut into squares.

NUTRITION FACTS (1 BROWNIE)			
Calories	240	Fat	12g
Protein	2g	Cholesterol	50mg
Carbohydrate	34g	Sodium	100mg

Cherry Sour Cream Bars

PREPARATION TIME: 15 minutes
BAKING TIME: 32 minutes

YIELD: 36 bars

CRUST
2   cups all-purpose flour
⅔   cup sugar
⅔   cup LAND O LAKES® Butter, softened

FILLING
1   (21-ounce) can cherry fruit filling
¾   cup LAND O LAKES® Sour Cream (Regular, Light or No•Fat)
2   teaspoons almond extract

TOPPING
2   cups flaked coconut
½   cup sliced almonds
2   tablespoons LAND O LAKES® Butter, melted

✤ Heat oven to 350°. In large mixer bowl combine all crust ingredients. Beat at low speed, scraping bowl often, until mixture resembles coarse crumbs (2 to 3 minutes). Press on bottom of 13x9-inch baking pan. Bake for 15 to 20 minutes or until golden brown around edges.

✤ Meanwhile, in medium bowl stir together all filling ingredients; spread over hot partially baked crust.

✤ In small bowl stir together all topping ingredients. Sprinkle topping evenly over filling. Continue baking for 17 to 20 minutes or until light golden brown. Cool completely; cut into bars. Store refrigerated.

NUTRITION FACTS (1 BAR)			
Calories	130	Fat	7g
Protein	1g	Cholesterol	15mg
Carbohydrate	16g	Sodium	55mg

OLD-WORLD RASPBERRY BARS

PREPARATION TIME: 15 minutes
BAKING TIME: 40 minutes

YIELD: 24 bars

CRUMB MIXTURE
2¼ cups all-purpose flour
1 cup sugar
1 cup chopped pecans
1 cup LAND O LAKES® Butter, softened
1 egg

FILLING
1 (10-ounce) jar raspberry preserves*

*Substitute 1 (10-ounce) jar of your favorite flavor preserves.

❖ Heat oven to 350°. In large mixer bowl combine all crumb mixture ingredients. Beat at low speed, scraping bowl often, until mixture is crumbly (2 to 3 minutes). Reserve 1½ cups crumb mixture; set aside.

❖ Press remaining crumb mixture on bottom of greased 8 or 9-inch square baking pan. Spread preserves to within ½ inch of edge. Crumble reserved mixture over preserves.

❖ Bake for 40 to 50 minutes or until lightly browned. Cool completely; cut into bars.

TIP
Cover and store in pan up to 5 days or freeze in plastic containers up to 1 month.

NUTRITION FACTS (1 BAR)			
Calories	210	Fat	11g
Protein	2g	Cholesterol	30mg
Carbohydrate	27g	Sodium	85mg

Lemon-Butter Bars

PREPARATION TIME: 30 minutes
BAKING TIME: 28 minutes

YIELD: 16 bars

CRUST
1⅓ cups all-purpose flour
¼ cup sugar
½ cup LAND O LAKES® Butter, softened

FILLING
¾ cup sugar
2 eggs
2 tablespoons all-purpose flour
¼ teaspoon baking powder
3 tablespoons lemon juice

Powdered sugar

❖ Heat oven to 350°. In small mixer bowl combine all crust ingredients. Beat at low speed, scraping bowl often, until mixture is crumbly (2 to 3 minutes). Press on bottom of 8-inch square baking pan. Bake for 15 to 20 minutes or until edges are lightly browned.

❖ Meanwhile, in small mixer bowl combine all filling ingredients except powdered sugar. Beat at low speed, scraping bowl often, until well mixed. Pour filling over hot partially baked crust. Continue baking for 18 to 20 minutes or until filling is set. Sprinkle with powdered sugar while still warm and again when cool. Cut into bars.

❖ Microwave Directions: Prepare crust as directed above. Press on bottom of 8-inch square baking dish. Microwave on HIGH until top looks dry (4 to 5 minutes). Meanwhile, in small microwave-safe mixer bowl combine all filling ingredients except powdered sugar. Beat at low speed, scraping bowl often, until well mixed. Microwave filling on HIGH, stirring every minute, until warm and slightly thickened (2 to 4 minutes). Pour over hot crust. Microwave on HIGH, turning dish ¼ turn after half the time, until filling is just set in center (2 to 5 minutes). Sprinkle with powdered sugar while still warm and again when cool. Cut into bars.

NUTRITION FACTS (1 BAR)			
Calories	150	Fat	6g
Protein	2g	Cholesterol	40mg
Carbohydrate	22g	Sodium	70mg

Snowball Cookies

PREPARATION TIME: 30 minutes
BAKING TIME: 18 minutes

YIELD: 3 dozen cookies

2 cups all-purpose flour
2 cups finely chopped pecans
¼ cup sugar
1 cup LAND O LAKES® Butter, softened
1 teaspoon vanilla

Powdered sugar

❖ Heat oven to 325°. In large mixer bowl combine all ingredients except powdered sugar. Beat at low speed, scraping bowl occasionally, until well mixed (2 to 3 minutes).

❖ Shape rounded teaspoonfuls of dough into 1-inch balls. Place 1 inch apart on cookie sheets. Bake for 18 to 25 minutes or until very lightly browned. Cool 5 minutes; roll in powdered sugar while still warm and again when cool.

NUTRITION FACTS (1 COOKIE)			
Calories	130	Fat	10g
Protein	1g	Cholesterol	15mg
Carbohydrate	11g	Sodium	50mg

TIP
Greasing cookie sheets is unnecessary for cookies such as these, which are made with a rich buttery dough. Only grease cookie sheets when specifically indicated in a recipe.

Grandma's Cookie Jar Oatmeal Cookies

PREPARATION TIME: 50 minutes BAKING TIME: 8 minutes

YIELD: 4 dozen cookies

3 cups quick-cooking oats
2 cups firmly packed brown sugar
1 cup LAND O LAKES® Butter, softened
2 eggs
1 teaspoon baking soda
1 teaspoon cinnamon
½ teaspoon salt
2 teaspoons vanilla
1¾ cups all-purpose flour
1½ cups raisins

✤ Heat oven to 375°. In large mixer bowl combine all ingredients except flour and raisins. Beat at low speed, scraping bowl often, until well mixed (1 to 2 minutes). Add flour; continue beating until well mixed (1 to 2 minutes). By hand, stir in raisins.

✤ Drop dough by rounded teaspoonfuls 2 inches apart onto greased cookie sheets. Bake for 8 to 10 minutes or until edges are lightly browned.

NUTRITION FACTS (1 COOKIE)			
Calories	120	Fat	4g
Protein	2g	Cholesterol	20mg
Carbohydrate	19g	Sodium	90mg

Butter Pecan Tartlets

PREPARATION TIME: 1 hour
BAKING TIME: 12 minutes   COOLING TIME: 20 minutes

YIELD: 3 dozen tartlets

TART SHELLS
1¾ cups all-purpose flour
½ cup LAND O LAKES® Butter, softened
½ cup sugar
1 egg
1 teaspoon almond extract

FILLING
1 cup powdered sugar
½ cup LAND O LAKES® Butter
⅓ cup dark corn syrup
1 cup chopped pecans

36 pecan halves

❖Heat oven to 400°. In large mixer bowl combine all tart shell ingredients. Beat at medium speed, scraping bowl often, until mixture is crumbly (2 to 3 minutes).

❖Press 1 tablespoon mixture into cups of mini muffin pans to form 36 (1¾ to 2-inch) shells. Bake for 7 to 10 minutes or until very lightly browned. Remove from oven. Reduce oven to 350°.

❖Meanwhile, in 2-quart saucepan combine all filling ingredients except chopped pecans and pecan halves. Cook over medium heat, stirring occasionally, until mixture comes to a full boil (4 to 5 minutes). Remove from heat; stir in chopped pecans.

❖Spoon into baked shells. Top each with pecan half. Bake for 5 minutes. Cool 20 minutes; remove from pans.

N U T R I T I O N F A C T S			
(1 TARTLET)			
Calories	130	Fat	8g
Protein	1g	Cholesterol	20mg
Carbohydrate	13g	Sodium	60mg

Tart n' Tangy Lemonade Frosties

PREPARATION TIME: 1 hour
BAKING TIME: 8 minutes   COOLING TIME: 15 minutes

YIELD: 4 dozen cookies

COOKIES
1¼ cups sugar
1¼ cups LAND O LAKES® Butter, softened
2 eggs
3 cups all-purpose flour
1 (6-ounce) can frozen lemonade or orange juice concentrate, thawed, reserve 2 tablespoons for frosting
1 teaspoon baking soda

FROSTING
3 cups powdered sugar
⅓ cup LAND O LAKES® Butter, softened
2 tablespoons reserved frozen lemonade concentrate
1 teaspoon vanilla
1 to 2 tablespoons milk

Yellow colored sugar, if desired

❖Heat oven to 400°. In large mixer bowl combine 1¼ cups sugar, butter and eggs. Beat at medium speed, scraping bowl often, until creamy (3 to 5 minutes). Reduce speed to low. Beat, gradually adding flour, lemonade concentrate and baking soda and scraping bowl often, until well mixed (1 to 2 minutes).

❖Drop dough by rounded teaspoonfuls onto cookie sheets. Bake for 8 to 14 minutes or until edges are lightly browned. Cool completely.

❖In small mixer bowl combine all frosting ingredients except milk and colored sugar. Beat at low speed, scraping bowl often and adding enough milk for desired spreading consistency. Frost cooled cookies; sprinkle with colored sugar.

N U T R I T I O N F A C T S			
(1 COOKIE)			
Calories	140	Fat	6g
Protein	1g	Cholesterol	25mg
Carbohydrate	20g	Sodium	90mg

Coconut Date Balls

PREPARATION TIME: 45 minutes
COOKING TIME: 8 minutes CHILLING TIME: 1 hour

YIELD: 4 dozen cookies

½ cup LAND O LAKES® Butter
1 cup sugar
1 (8-ounce) package chopped dates
1 egg, slightly beaten
½ teaspoon salt
2 tablespoons milk
1 teaspoon vanilla
2 cups crushed cornflakes
½ cup chopped pecans
½ cup chopped maraschino cherries, drained
1½ cups flaked coconut

❖In 10-inch skillet melt butter over medium heat (3 to 4 minutes). Stir in sugar and dates. Remove from heat; stir in egg, salt, milk and vanilla.

❖Cook over medium heat, stirring occasionally, until mixture comes to a full boil (4 to 7 minutes). Boil, stirring constantly, 1 minute. Remove from heat; stir in cornflakes, pecans and cherries.

❖Shape into 1-inch balls; roll in coconut. Place on waxed paper. Cover; refrigerate until set (at least 1 hour).

❖Microwave Directions: In 2-quart casserole melt butter on HIGH (1 to 1½ minutes). Stir in sugar, dates, egg, salt, milk and vanilla. Microwave on HIGH, stirring every minute, until mixture comes to a full boil (2½ to 4 minutes). Microwave on HIGH 1 minute. Stir in cornflakes, pecans and cherries. Shape into 1-inch balls; roll in coconut. Place on waxed paper. Refrigerate until set (at least 1 hour).

NUTRITION FACTS (1 COOKIE)			
Calories	90	Fat	4g
Protein	1g	Cholesterol	10mg
Carbohydrate	13g	Sodium	80mg

Sour Cream n' Raisin Cookies

PREPARATION TIME: 1 hour
CHILLING TIME: 2 hours BAKING TIME: 10 minutes

YIELD: 4½ dozen cookies

2½ cups all-purpose flour
1 cup sugar
½ cup LAND O LAKES® Light or No•Fat Sour Cream
½ cup LAND O LAKES® Butter, softened
2 eggs, slightly beaten
2 teaspoons ground nutmeg
½ teaspoon baking soda
½ teaspoon salt
1 cup raisins

❖In large mixer bowl combine all ingredients except 1 cup flour and raisins. Beat at medium speed, scraping bowl often, until smooth (2 to 3 minutes). By hand, stir in remaining flour and raisins until well mixed. Cover; refrigerate at least 2 hours.

❖Heat oven to 350°. Drop dough by teaspoonfuls 2 inches apart onto greased cookie sheets. Bake for 10 to 12 minutes or until lightly browned.

NUTRITION FACTS (1 COOKIE)			
Calories	60	Fat	2g
Protein	1g	Cholesterol	15mg
Carbohydrate	11g	Sodium	50mg

Versatile Butter Cookies

PREPARATION TIME: 1 hour
BAKING TIME: 7 minutes

YIELD: 5 dozen cookies

1½ cups sugar
1 cup LAND O LAKES® Butter, softened
2 eggs
3 cups all-purpose flour
1 teaspoon baking soda
1 teaspoon vanilla

❖ Heat oven to 400°. In large mixer bowl combine sugar, butter and eggs. Beat at medium speed, scraping bowl often, until creamy (3 to 5 minutes). Reduce speed to low; add all remaining ingredients. Beat, scraping bowl often, until well mixed (1 to 2 minutes).

❖ Divide dough in half; prepare desired variations using half of dough for each variation. Bake for 7 to 10 minutes or until edges are lightly browned.

VARIATIONS

❖ Cherry Chocolate Bits: By hand, stir in ¼ cup chopped or grated semi-sweet chocolate. Shape rounded teaspoonfuls of dough into 1-inch balls. Place 2 inches apart on cookie sheets. Press 1 drained maraschino cherry half into center of each ball.

❖ Cinnamon N' Sugar: Shape rounded teaspoonfuls of dough into 1-inch balls; dip in mixture of 2 tablespoons sugar and 2 teaspoons cinnamon or colored sugar. Place 2 inches apart on cookie sheets.

❖ Coconut Balls: By hand, stir in ½ cup flaked coconut. Shape rounded teaspoonfuls of dough into 1-inch balls. Place 2 inches apart on cookie sheets. After baking, dip in powdered sugar to coat.

❖ Spice Drops: Shape rounded teaspoonfuls of dough into 1-inch balls. Place 2 inches apart on cookie sheets. Press cut spice gumdrops into each ball.

RASPBERRY ALMOND SHORTBREAD THUMBPRINTS

PREPARATION TIME: 45 minutes BAKING TIME: 14 minutes

YIELD: 3½ dozen cookies

COOKIES
⅔ cup sugar
1 cup LAND O LAKES® Butter, softened
½ teaspoon almond extract
2 cups all-purpose flour

½ cup raspberry jam*

GLAZE
1 cup powdered sugar
1½ teaspoons almond extract
2 to 3 teaspoons water

*Substitute ½ cup of your favorite flavor jam.

✤ Heat oven to 350°. In large mixer bowl combine sugar, butter and almond extract. Beat at medium speed, scraping bowl often, until creamy (2 to 3 minutes). Reduce speed to low; add flour. Beat, scraping bowl often, until well mixed (2 to 3 minutes).

✤ Shape dough into 1-inch balls. Place 2 inches apart on cookie sheets. With thumb, make indentation in center of each cookie (edges may crack slightly). Fill each indentation with about ¼ teaspoon jam. Bake for 14 to 18 minutes or until edges are lightly browned. Let stand 1 minute; remove from cookie sheets.

✤ In small bowl stir together powdered sugar, 1½ teaspoons almond extract and enough water for glazing consistency. Drizzle over cookies. Cool completely.

NUTRITION FACTS (1 COOKIE)			
Calories	90	Fat	4g
Protein	1g	Cholesterol	10mg
Carbohydrate	13g	Sodium	45mg

Old-Fashioned Chewy Molasses Cookies

PREPARATION TIME: 30 minutes   CHILLING TIME: 2 hours   BAKING TIME: 14 minutes

YIELD: 4½ dozen cookies

4½ cups all-purpose flour
2 cups sugar
1 cup LAND O LAKES® Butter, softened
1 cup molasses
½ cup milk
2 eggs
1 teaspoon baking soda
1 teaspoon ground ginger
½ teaspoon cinnamon
¼ teaspoon salt

Sugar

 In large mixer bowl combine all ingredients <u>except</u> additional sugar. Beat at low speed, scraping bowl often, until well mixed (2 to 3 minutes). Cover; refrigerate until firm (at least 2 hours).

 Heat oven to 350°. Shape rounded tablespoonfuls of dough into balls; roll in sugar. Place 2 inches apart on cookie sheets. Bake for 14 to 16 minutes or until slightly firm to the touch.

NUTRITION FACTS		
(1 COOKIE)		
Calories	120	Fat	4g
Protein	1g	Cholesterol	20mg
Carbohydrate	20g	Sodium	70mg

Tip

Either light or dark molasses may be used in this recipe. Dark molasses is darker and thicker than light, with a stronger, less sweet flavor.
Do not use blackstrap molasses.

Jumbo Candy & Nut Cookies

PREPARATION TIME: 45 minutes
BAKING TIME: 13 minutes

YIELD: 2 dozen cookies

1 cup sugar
1 cup firmly packed brown sugar
1 cup LAND O LAKES® Butter, softened
2 eggs
1 tablespoon vanilla
2 cups all-purpose flour
1½ cups quick-cooking oats
1 teaspoon baking soda
½ teaspoon salt
1 (16-ounce) bag (2 cups) candy coated milk chocolate pieces
1 cup coarsely chopped peanuts

 Heat oven to 350°. In large mixer bowl combine sugar, brown sugar, butter, eggs and vanilla. Beat at medium speed, scraping bowl often, until creamy (2 to 3 minutes). Reduce speed to low; add all remaining ingredients <u>except</u> candy and peanuts. Beat, scraping bowl often, until well mixed (2 to 3 minutes). By hand, stir in candy and peanuts.

 Drop dough by scant ¼ cupfuls 2 inches apart onto greased cookie sheets. Bake for 13 to 16 minutes or until light golden brown.

NUTRITION FACTS		
(1 COOKIE)		
Calories	330	Fat	18g
Protein	5g	Cholesterol	40mg
Carbohydrate	41g	Sodium	200mg

Favorite Butter Cookies

PREPARATION TIME: 1 hour 30 minutes
CHILLING TIME: 2 hours BAKING TIME: 6 minutes COOLING TIME: 15 minutes

YIELD: 3 dozen cookies

COOKIES
2½ cups all-purpose flour
1 cup sugar
1 cup LAND O LAKES® Butter, softened
1 egg
1 teaspoon baking powder
2 tablespoons orange juice
1 tablespoon vanilla

FROSTING
4 cups powdered sugar
½ cup LAND O LAKES® Butter, softened
2 teaspoons vanilla
3 to 4 tablespoons milk

DECORATIONS
   Colored sugars
   Flaked coconut
   Cinnamon candies

❖In large mixer bowl combine all cookie ingredients. Beat at low speed, scraping bowl often, until well mixed (1 to 2 minutes). Cover; refrigerate until firm (at least 2 hours).

❖Heat oven to 400°. On lightly floured surface roll out dough, one-third at a time (keeping remaining dough refrigerated), to ¼-inch thickness. Cut with 3-inch cookie cutters. Place 1 inch apart on cookie sheets. If desired, sprinkle colored sugars on some of the cookies or bake and decorate later. Bake for 6 to 10 minutes or until edges are lightly browned. Cool completely.

❖In small mixer bowl combine all frosting ingredients except milk. Beat at low speed, gradually adding enough milk for desired spreading consistency. Frost or decorate cooled cookies.

TIP
To use cookies as ornaments, while cookies are still warm use toothpick to make hole in top of each cookie. Cool and decorate. Thread ribbon or thread through holes in cookies.

NUTRITION FACTS (1 COOKIE)			
Calories	170	Fat	8g
Protein	1g	Cholesterol	25mg
Carbohydrate	23g	Sodium	90mg

Cinnamon n' Sugar Shortbread

PREPARATION TIME: 30 minutes
BAKING TIME: 20 minutes

YIELD: 16 cookies

SHORTBREAD

1¾ cups all-purpose flour
¾ cup powdered sugar
½ cup cake flour
1 cup LAND O LAKES® Butter, softened
½ teaspoon cinnamon

TOPPING

1 tablespoon sugar
⅛ teaspoon cinnamon

❖ Heat oven to 350°. In large bowl combine all shortbread ingredients. With fork, stir together until soft dough forms. Press evenly on bottom of 2 (9-inch) shortbread molds. Prick all over with a fork.

❖ Bake for 20 to 30 minutes or until light golden brown. Cool in pan 10 minutes. Loosen edges of shortbread from pan with knife; invert onto wooden board.

❖ In small bowl stir together topping ingredients; sprinkle over shortbread. Cut into wedges.

Tip

*Two (9-inch) pie pans can be used in place of
2 (9-inch) shortbread molds.
Sprinkle with topping. Score each pan into 8 wedges;
prick all over with fork. Bake as directed above.
Cool on wire rack; cut into wedges.*

NUTRITION FACTS (1 COOKIE)			
Calories	190	Fat	12g
Protein	2g	Cholesterol	30mg
Carbohydrate	19g	Sodium	120mg

*L*uscious fillings surrounded by crusts made with LAND O LAKES® Butter make these pies real show stoppers. A slice of homemade pie served with a glass of cold milk after school or with hot coffee after a great dinner is like a little slice of heaven!

Fresh Raspberry Cream Cheese Pie

PREPARATION TIME: 45 minutes
BAKING TIME: 10 minutes CHILLING TIME: 2 hours 30 minutes

YIELD: 8 servings

CRUST
1¼ cups graham
cracker crumbs
¼ cup sugar
⅓ cup LAND O LAKES®
Butter, melted

FILLING
1 (10-ounce) pack-
age frozen rasp-
berries in syrup,
thawed
1 (¼-ounce) enve-
lope unflavored
gelatin
¼ cup water
¼ cup sugar
2 tablespoons rasp-
berry-flavored
liqueur or water
½ cup powdered
sugar
1 (8-ounce) pack-
age cream cheese
or light cream
cheese
1 cup whipping
cream, whipped
2 (6-ounce) con-
tainers fresh rasp-
berries, washed,
drained,
reserve ½ cup

❖Heat oven to 350°. In medium bowl stir together all crust ingredients. Press on bottom and up sides of 9-inch pie pan. Bake for 10 to 12 minutes or until lightly browned; cool completely.

❖In 5-cup blender container place raspberries and syrup. Cover; blend on high speed until pureed (1 minute). Strain sauce to remove seeds.

❖In 1-quart saucepan sprinkle gelatin over water; let stand 5 minutes to soften. Cook over low heat until gelatin is dissolved (1 to 2 minutes). Remove from heat; stir in raspberry puree, ¼ cup sugar and liqueur. Cover; refrigerate until mixture mounds when dropped from spoon (30 to 40 minutes).

❖In small mixer bowl beat powdered sugar and cream cheese until smooth (1 to 2 minutes). Gently stir in 1 cup whipped cream. Spread cream cheese mixture into cooled crust. Arrange raspberries over cream cheese mixture. Pour gelatin mixture over raspberries, spreading to cover. Cover; refrigerate until gelatin is set (2 to 3 hours). Using pastry bag, pipe remaining whipped cream onto pie and garnish with reserved fresh raspberries, if desired.

NUTRITION FACTS		
(1 SERVING)		
Calories	470	Fat	30g
Protein	5g	Cholesterol	90mg
Carbohydrate	46g	Sodium	260mg

CHERRY ORCHARD PIE

PREPARATION TIME: 45 minutes
BAKING TIME: 50 minutes

YIELD: 8 servings

CRUST

2 cups all-purpose flour
¼ teaspoon salt
⅔ cup LAND O LAKES® Butter, chilled
4 to 5 tablespoons cold water

FILLING

1 cup sugar
⅓ cup all-purpose flour
⅛ teaspoon salt
2 (16-ounce) cans red tart pitted cherries, drained
1 teaspoon grated orange peel

Milk
Sugar

❖Heat oven to 400°. In large bowl stir together 2 cups flour and ¼ teaspoon salt; cut in butter until crumbly. With fork, mix in water until flour is just moistened.

❖Divide pastry in half; shape each half into a ball. Wrap 1 ball in plastic food wrap; refrigerate. On lightly floured surface roll other ball into 12-inch circle. Place in 9-inch pie pan. Trim pastry to ½ inch from rim of pan; set aside.

❖In large bowl combine sugar, ⅓ cup flour and ⅛ teaspoon salt. Add cherries and orange peel; toss lightly to coat. Spoon into prepared crust. With remaining half of pastry prepare lattice top. Roll remaining pastry ball into 11-inch circle. With sharp knife or pastry wheel, cut circle into 10 (½-inch) strips. Place 5 strips, 1 inch apart, across filling in pie pan. Place remaining 5 strips, 1 inch apart, at right angles to the strips already in place. With kitchen shears, trim strips. Fold trimmed edge of bottom pastry over strips; build up an edge. Seal; crimp or flute edge. Brush strips with milk; sprinkle with sugar. Cover edge of crust with 2-inch strip of aluminum foil.

❖Bake for 50 to 60 minutes or until crust is golden brown and filling bubbles in center. If desired, remove aluminum foil during last 5 minutes. If browning too quickly, shield lattice strips with aluminum foil.

NUTRITION FACTS			
(1 SERVING)			
Calories	420	Fat	16g
Protein	5g	Cholesterol	41mg
Carbohydrate	68g	Sodium	260mg

COUNTRY APPLE CUSTARD PIE

PREPARATION TIME: 30 minutes
BAKING TIME: 35 minutes

YIELD: 8 servings

CRUST
Single crust pie
pastry

FILLING
1 cup sugar
1 cup LAND O LAKES®
Sour Cream
(Regular, Light or
No•Fat)
2 eggs, beaten
2 tablespoons all-
purpose flour
¼ teaspoon salt
1 teaspoon vanilla
3 medium (3 cups)
tart cooking
apples, peeled,
cored, coarsely
chopped

STREUSEL
3 tablespoons
LAND O LAKES®
Butter
¼ cup all-purpose
flour
¼ cup firmly packed
brown sugar

❖Heat oven to 375°. Place pastry in 9-inch
pie pan. Crimp or flute crust; set aside.

❖In large bowl combine sugar, sour cream,
eggs, 2 tablespoons flour, salt and vanilla;
stir in apples. Pour into crust.

❖In 1-quart saucepan melt butter; stir in
¼ cup flour and brown sugar. Crumble over
pie. Bake for 35 to 45 minutes or until filling
is set. Cool completely on rack. Store
refrigerated.

TIP

*If crust is browning too quickly,
shield with aluminum foil.*

NUTRITION FACTS (1 SERVING)			
Calories	380	Fat	15g
Protein	4g	Cholesterol	80mg
Carbohydrate	58g	Sodium	280mg

BLUEBERRY RHUBARB TART

PREPARATION TIME: 30 minutes
BAKING TIME: 50 minutes

YIELD: 8 servings

CRUST
1 cup all-purpose
flour
1 tablespoon sugar
¼ teaspoon salt
¼ cup LAND O LAKES®
Butter, chilled
¼ cup shortening
3 tablespoons cold
water

FILLING
½ cup sugar
3 tablespoons
cornstarch
2 cups sliced ¼-
inch fresh or
frozen rhubarb
⅔ cup apple juice
1 cup fresh or
frozen blueberries

Sweetened
whipped cream,
if desired

❖Heat oven to 375°. In medium bowl stir
together flour, 1 tablespoon sugar and salt;
cut in butter and shortening until crumbly.
With fork, mix in water until flour is just
moistened. Shape into a ball.

❖On lightly floured surface roll ball into
10-inch circle. Place in 9-inch tart pan with
removable bottom; press on bottom and up
sides of pan. Bake for 10 minutes.

❖Meanwhile, in 2-quart saucepan combine
½ cup sugar and cornstarch. Gradually stir
in rhubarb and apple juice. Cook over medium heat, stirring constantly, until thickened
(5 to 7 minutes). Remove from heat; stir in
blueberries.

❖Pour into crust. Bake for 40 to 50 minutes
or until center is bubbly. Cool completely.

❖Using pastry bag, pipe whipped cream onto
tart forming a lattice.

NUTRITION FACTS (1 SERVING)			
Calories	280	Fat	15g
Protein	42g	Cholesterol	25mg
Carbohydrate	36g	Sodium	130mg

Choco-Peanut Butter Ice Cream Pie

PREPARATION TIME: 20 minutes BAKING TIME: 6 minutes
COOLING TIME: 30 minutes FREEZING TIME: 5 hours

YIELD: 8 servings

CRUST

1½ cups graham cracker crumbs
3 tablespoons sugar
2 tablespoons chopped salted peanuts
¼ cup LAND O LAKES® Butter, melted

FILLING

2 cups chocolate ice cream, softened slightly
4 cups vanilla ice cream, softened slightly
⅓ cup peanut butter
2 tablespoons chopped salted peanuts

Chocolate-flavored syrup

TIP

Do not use an 8-inch pie pan.

❖ Heat oven to 350°. In small bowl stir together all crust ingredients. Press on bottom and up sides of 9-inch or 10-inch pie pan. Bake for 6 to 8 minutes or until lightly browned. Cool completely.

❖ Spread softened chocolate ice cream over bottom of cooled pie crust. Freeze until firm (about 30 minutes).

❖ In large mixer bowl combine vanilla ice cream and peanut butter. Beat at low speed, scraping bowl often, until peanut butter is evenly distributed. Freeze until ice cream and peanut butter mixture holds soft mounds (30 to 45 minutes).

❖ Spoon ice cream and peanut butter mixture over chocolate ice cream layer. Spread to edges of crust, mounding slightly higher in center. Sprinkle with 2 tablespoons chopped peanuts. Freeze for 4 to 5 hours or until firm.

❖ Let stand at room temperature 5 minutes before serving; drizzle with chocolate syrup.

Chocolate-Laced Pecan Pie

PREPARATION TIME: 30 minutes
BAKING TIME: 40 minutes   CHILLING TIME: 4 hours

YIELD: 8 servings

CRUST
Single crust pie
pastry

FILLING
⅔ cup sugar
⅓ cup LAND O LAKES®
    Butter, melted
1 cup light corn
    syrup
3 eggs
½ teaspoon salt
1 cup pecan halves
½ cup semi-sweet
    real chocolate
    chips

❖Heat oven to 375˚. Place pastry in 9-inch pie pan. Crimp or flute crust; set aside.

❖In small mixer bowl combine sugar, butter, corn syrup, eggs and salt. Beat at medium speed, scraping bowl often, until well mixed (1 to 2 minutes). By hand, stir in pecans and chocolate chips. Pour into prepared pie crust. If desired, turn pecan halves right side up. Cover pie loosely with aluminum foil.

❖Bake for 30 minutes. Remove aluminum foil; continue baking for 10 to 15 minutes or until filling is set. If browning too quickly, re-cover with aluminum foil. Cool; refrigerate at least 4 hours or until ready to serve.

❖If desired, dip additional pecan halves halfway in melted chocolate chips; refrigerate until set. Serve pie with sweetened whipped cream and garnish with dipped pecan halves, if desired.

TIP
If desired, omit semi-sweet real chocolate chips for a traditional pecan pie.

Maple Pecan Pumpkin Pie

PREPARATION TIME: 45 minutes
BAKING TIME: 55 minutes

YIELD: 8 servings

CRUST
1 cup all-purpose
    flour
⅛ teaspoon salt
⅓ cup LAND O LAKES®
    Butter, chilled
2 to 3 tablespoons
    cold water

FILLING
1 (15-ounce) can
    (1¾ cups) pump-
    kin
¼ cup sugar
2 eggs, slightly
    beaten
1 cup whipping
    cream
¼ cup pure maple
    syrup or maple-
    flavored syrup
2 teaspoons pump-
    kin pie spice

TOPPING
½ cup pecan halves
3 tablespoons pure
    maple syrup or
    maple-flavored
    syrup
½ cup whipping
    cream, chilled

❖Heat oven to 375˚. In large bowl stir together flour and salt; cut in butter until crumbly. With fork, mix in water until flour is just moistened. Shape into a ball. On lightly floured surface roll ball into 12-inch circle. Place in 9-inch pie pan. Crimp or flute crust; set aside.

❖In large bowl stir together pumpkin, sugar and eggs. Stir in all remaining filling ingredients. Pour into prepared pie crust. Cover edge of crust with 2-inch strip of aluminum foil. Bake for 40 minutes. Remove aluminum foil. Continue baking for 15 to 25 minutes or until knife inserted in center comes out clean.

❖Arrange pecan halves on top of pie; drizzle or brush 1 tablespoon maple syrup over pecans.

❖In chilled small mixer bowl beat whipping cream at high speed until soft peaks form. Gradually add remaining maple syrup; continue beating until stiff peaks form (1 to 2 minutes). Serve with pie.

Coconut Banana-Cream Pie

PREPARATION TIME: 45 minutes
BAKING TIME: 37 minutes   COOLING TIME: 30 minutes   CHILLING TIME: 3 hours

YIELD: 8 servings

CRUST
1 (7-ounce) package (2⅔ cups) flaked coconut
¼ cup LAND O LAKES® Butter, melted

FILLING
½ cup sugar
¼ cup all-purpose flour
¼ teaspoon salt
2 cups milk
3 eggs, separated
1 teaspoon vanilla
1 medium banana, sliced

MERINGUE
3 reserved egg whites
6 tablespoons sugar

❖ Heat oven to 325°. Reserve ¼ cup coconut; set aside.

❖ In medium bowl stir together remaining coconut and butter; press on bottom and up sides of 9-inch pie pan. Bake for 20 to 25 minutes or until golden brown.

❖ Meanwhile, in 2-quart saucepan combine ½ cup sugar, flour and salt; stir in milk. Cook over medium heat, stirring constantly, until mixture comes to a full boil (7 to 8 minutes). Remove from heat. Stir small amount of milk mixture into egg yolks; return to pan. Reduce heat to low. Continue cooking until slightly thickened (1 to 2 minutes). DO NOT BOIL. Stir in vanilla. Pour <u>half</u> of warm filling into baked crust; cover with banana slices. Top with remaining filling.

❖ Heat oven to 375°. In small mixer bowl beat egg whites at high speed until foamy (1 to 2 minutes). Continue beating, gradually adding 6 tablespoons sugar, until stiff and glossy (1 to 2 minutes). Spread onto warm filling, sealing to edge of crust. Sprinkle with reserved coconut.

❖ Bake for 9 to 11 minutes or until lightly browned. Cool 30 minutes at room temperature. Refrigerate at least 3 hours. Store refrigerated.

NUTRITION FACTS (1 SERVING)			
Calories	340	Fat	17g
Protein	6g	Cholesterol	100mg
Carbohydrate	43g	Sodium	240mg

CHEWY CARAMEL-BROWNIE PIE

PREPARATION TIME: 30 minutes
BAKING TIME: 23 minutes STANDING TIME: 30 minutes

YIELD: 8 servings

BROWNIE
½ cup LAND O LAKES® Butter
2 (1-ounce) squares unsweetened baking chocolate
1 cup sugar
¾ cup all-purpose flour
2 eggs, slightly beaten
½ teaspoon baking powder
½ teaspoon salt
1 teaspoon vanilla

CARAMEL
8 ounces (30) caramels,
unwrapped
3 tablespoons whipping cream
½ cup chopped pecans
¼ cup semi-sweet chocolate
chips

Vanilla ice cream, if desired

❖Heat oven to 350°. In 2-quart saucepan melt butter and unsweetened chocolate over medium heat, stirring occasionally (4 to 6 minutes). Stir in all remaining brownie ingredients.

❖Spread batter into greased 9-inch pie pan. Bake for 20 to 25 minutes or until brownie is firm to the touch.

❖Meanwhile, in 1-quart saucepan melt caramels and whipping cream over medium-low heat, stirring occasionally, until smooth (5 to 6 minutes). Remove brownie from oven; spread melted caramel mixture over entire baked brownie. Sprinkle with pecans and chocolate chips.

❖Continue baking for 3 to 5 minutes or until caramel mixture is bubbly. Let stand 30 to 45 minutes; cut into wedges. Serve warm with ice cream.

TIP
This brownie crust should not be overbaked.
To determine doneness the center should be firm to the touch.
Another way to determine brownie doneness is
to insert a toothpick in the center; it will come out with
a few moist crumbs on it.

NUTRITION FACTS (1 SERVING)			
Calories	640	Fat	36g
Protein	8g	Cholesterol	120mg
Carbohydrate	79g	Sodium	410mg

BLACK FOREST PIE

PREPARATION TIME: 45 minutes
BAKING TIME: 40 minutes   CHILLING TIME: 2 hours

YIELD: 10 servings

CRUST
Single crust pie pastry

FILLING
¾ cup LAND O LAKES® Butter
¾ cup sugar
6 tablespoons unsweetened cocoa
⅔ cup ground blanched almonds
2 tablespoons all-purpose flour
3 eggs, separated
2 tablespoons water
¼ cup sugar

TOPPING
⅓ cup LAND O LAKES® Light or No•Fat Sour Cream
2 tablespoons sugar
½ teaspoon vanilla

1 cup canned cherry pie filling

GLAZE
½ cup semi-sweet real chocolate chips
1½ teaspoons shortening

❖Heat oven to 350°. Place pastry in 9-inch pie pan. Crimp or flute crust; set aside.

❖In 2-quart saucepan melt ¾ cup butter over medium heat (3 to 5 minutes). Stir in ¾ cup sugar and 6 tablespoons cocoa. Remove from heat; cool 5 minutes. Stir in almonds and flour. Stir in egg yolks, 1 at a time, until well mixed. Stir in 2 tablespoons water.

❖In small mixer bowl beat egg whites at high speed, scraping bowl often, until foamy. Continue beating, gradually adding ¼ cup sugar, until soft peaks form (30 to 60 seconds). Fold chocolate mixture into egg whites just until blended.

❖Pour mixture into prepared pie crust. Bake for 35 to 45 minutes or until toothpick inserted in center comes out clean. Cool 5 minutes.

❖In medium bowl stir together all topping ingredients except cherry pie filling. Spread over warm pie; top with spoonfuls of cherry pie filling. Continue baking pie for 5 minutes.

❖In 1-quart saucepan melt chocolate chips and shortening over low heat, stirring constantly, until melted (2 to 3 minutes). Drizzle over pie. Refrigerate at least 2 hours.

NUTRITION FACTS (1 SERVING)			
Calories	460	Fat	30g
Protein	6g	Cholesterol	120mg
Carbohydrate	47g	Sodium	280mg

Fresh Fruit Tart

PREPARATION TIME: 1 hour
BAKING TIME: 13 minutes

YIELD: 10 servings

CRUST
½ cup LAND O LAKES®
   Butter, softened
⅓ cup sugar
1¼ cups all-purpose
   flour
2 tablespoons milk
½ teaspoon almond
   extract

FILLING
1 cup LAND O LAKES®
   Sour Cream
   (Regular, Light or
   No•Fat)
1 tablespoon sugar

TOPPING
½ cup shredded
   coconut
   Variety of your
   favorite fruits,
   cut up

❖Heat oven to 400°. In large mixer bowl combine butter and ⅓ cup sugar. Beat at medium speed, scraping bowl often, until creamy (1 to 2 minutes). Reduce speed to low. Add flour, milk and almond extract; beat until well mixed.

❖Press dough on bottom and up sides of 10-inch tart pan with removable bottom or 12-inch pizza pan; prick with fork. Bake for 13 to 20 minutes or until light golden brown. Cool completely.

❖In small bowl stir together sour cream and sugar; spread over cooled crust.

❖When ready to serve, sprinkle with coconut; arrange fruit on top. Store refrigerated.

Blueberry Sour Cream Pie

PREPARATION TIME: 15 minutes BAKING TIME: 10 minutes
COOLING TIME: 30 minutes CHILLING TIME: 1 hour

YIELD: 8 servings

CRUST
1½ cups graham cracker crumbs
⅓ cup LAND O LAKES® Butter, melted

FILLING
1 cup LAND O LAKES® Light or No•Fat Sour Cream
1¼ cups skim milk
1 (3.4-ounce) package vanilla instant pudding and pie filling mix*
1 cup fresh blueberries**

* Substitute 1 (0.9-ounce) package vanilla sugar-free instant pudding and pie filling.

**Substitute your favorite fresh fruit.

❖ Heat oven to 350°. In medium bowl stir together graham cracker crumbs and butter. Press on bottom and sides of 9-inch pie pan. Bake for 10 to 12 minutes or until lightly browned. Cool completely.

❖ In small mixer bowl place sour cream; beat at medium speed, gradually adding milk, until smooth (1 to 2 minutes). Continue beating, gradually adding pudding and scraping bowl often, until well mixed and thickened (1 to 2 minutes).

❖ Pour into baked crust. Refrigerate until set (1 to 2 hours). Garnish with blueberries.

NUTRITION FACTS			
(1 SERVING)			
Calories	240	Fat	11g
Protein	4g	Cholesterol	28mg
Carbohydrate	32g	Sodium	420mg

Chocolate Silk Pie

PREPARATION TIME: 30 minutes
CHILLING TIME: 3 hours

YIELD: 8 servings

CRUST
1½ cups (about 18) finely crushed chocolate sandwich cookies
¼ cup LAND O LAKES® Butter, melted

FILLING
1 cup sugar
¾ cup LAND O LAKES® Butter, softened
3 (1-ounce) squares semi-sweet baking chocolate, melted, cooled
¾ cup refrigerated egg substitute

Sweetened whipped cream, if desired
Chocolate curls, if desired

❖ In medium bowl stir together all crust ingredients. Press on bottom and up sides of 9-inch pie pan. Refrigerate 10 minutes.

❖ In small mixer bowl combine sugar and ¾ cup butter. Beat at medium speed, scraping bowl often, until well mixed (1 to 2 minutes). Add chocolate. Continue beating, scraping bowl often, until well mixed (1 to 2 minutes). Add egg substitute. Continue beating, scraping bowl often, until light and fluffy (4 minutes).

❖ Spoon into prepared crust. Refrigerate at least 3 hours or until set. Garnish with sweetened whipped cream and chocolate curls. Store refrigerated.

NUTRITION FACTS			
(1 SERVING)			
Calories	490	Fat	34g
Protein	4g	Cholesterol	90mg
Carbohydrate	47g	Sodium	390mg

LIME MERINGUE PIE

PREPARATION TIME: 40 minutes BAKING TIME: 24 minutes
COOKING TIME: 12 minutes COOLING TIME: 1 hour CHILLING TIME: 1 hour

YIELD: 8 servings

CRUST
1 cup all-purpose flour
⅛ teaspoon salt
3 tablespoons LAND O LAKES® Butter, chilled
2 tablespoons shortening
2 to 3 tablespoons cold water

FILLING
1¼ cups sugar
⅓ cup cornstarch
¼ teaspoon salt
1¼ cups water
4 egg yolks, beaten
½ cup fresh lime juice
3 tablespoons LAND O LAKES® Butter
2 teaspoons grated lime peel

MERINGUE
4 egg whites
½ teaspoon cream of tartar
⅓ cup sugar

❖Heat oven to 475°. In large bowl stir together flour and salt; cut in butter and shortening until crumbly. With fork, mix in water. Shape into ball.

❖On lightly floured surface roll pastry into 12-inch circle. Trim pastry to 1 inch from edge of pan; crimp or flute edge. With fork, prick bottom and sides of pastry. Bake for 8 to 10 minutes or until lightly browned. Cool; set aside.

❖Reduce oven to 350°. Meanwhile, in 2-quart saucepan combine sugar, cornstarch and salt. Gradually stir in water. Cook over medium heat, stirring constantly, until mixture comes to a full boil. Boil 1 minute. With wire whisk, gradually stir ½ cup sugar mixture into beaten egg yolks. Gradually stir egg mixture into remaining hot mixture. Continue cooking, stirring constantly, until mixture thickens (5 to 7 minutes). Whisk in lime juice, butter and lime peel. Pour hot filling mixture into crust.

❖In large mixer bowl beat egg whites and cream of tartar at high speed until soft peaks form. Continue beating, gradually adding ⅓ cup sugar, until stiff peaks form (3 to 4 minutes). Spread meringue over filling, sealing meringue to crust edge. Bake for 10 to 15 minutes or until meringue is lightly browned. Cool at room temperature for 1 to 2 hours. Refrigerate at least 1 hour before serving. Store refrigerated.

40

MACADAMIA TART

PREPARATION TIME: 45 minutes CHILLING TIME: 1 hour 30 minutes
BAKING TIME: 28 minutes COOLING TIME: 1 hour

YIELD: 10 servings

CRUST
1 cup all-purpose flour
1 tablespoon sugar
¼ teaspoon salt
½ cup LAND O LAKES® Butter, chilled
2 to 3 tablespoons cold water

FILLING
1 cup firmly packed brown sugar
1 tablespoon all-purpose flour
1⅓ cups whipping cream
½ cup coarsely chopped macadamia nuts

GLAZE
2 tablespoons semi-sweet real chocolate chips
½ teaspoon shortening
Macadamia nuts, if desired

❖In medium bowl stir together 1 cup flour, sugar and salt; cut in butter until crumbly. With fork, mix in water until flour is just moistened. Shape into a ball; wrap in plastic food wrap. Refrigerate 30 minutes.

❖Heat oven to 425°. On lightly floured surface roll ball into 11-inch circle. Place in 10-inch tart pan with removable bottom. Press pastry on bottom and up sides of pan; crimp edge, trimming if needed. With fork, prick bottom and sides of pastry. Bake for 8 to 10 minutes or until just beginning to brown.

❖In medium bowl stir together brown sugar and 1 tablespoon flour until well blended. Gradually stir in whipping cream. Pour into crust; sprinkle with ½ cup nuts. Bake for 20 to 25 minutes or until filling is bubbly all over. Cool completely (1 to 2 hours).

❖In 1-quart saucepan melt chocolate chips and shortening over low heat, stirring constantly, until melted (1 to 2 minutes). Drizzle over tart. Garnish with nuts. Refrigerate at least 1 hour or overnight. Let stand at room temperature 15 minutes before serving.

Blue Ribbon Apple Pie

PREPARATION TIME: 1 hour BAKING TIME: 50 minutes COOLING TIME: 30 minutes

YIELD: 8 servings

CRUST

2 cups all-purpose flour
1 teaspoon sugar
¼ teaspoon salt
¼ teaspoon cinnamon
¼ teaspoon ground nutmeg
⅓ cup LAND O LAKES® Butter, chilled
⅓ cup shortening
4 to 5 tablespoons cold water

FILLING

½ cup sugar
¼ cup firmly packed brown sugar
¼ cup all-purpose flour
½ teaspoon cinnamon
½ teaspoon ground nutmeg
6 medium (6 cups) tart cooking apples, peeled, sliced ¼ inch

1 tablespoon LAND O LAKES® Butter
1 teaspoon sugar

❖ Heat oven to 400°. In large bowl stir together 2 cups flour, 1 teaspoon sugar, salt, ¼ teaspoon cinnamon and ¼ teaspoon nutmeg; cut in ⅓ cup butter and shortening until crumbly. With fork, mix in water until flour is just moistened.

❖ Divide pastry in half; shape each half into a ball. Wrap 1 ball in plastic food wrap; refrigerate. On lightly floured surface roll other ball into 12-inch circle. Place in 9-inch pie pan. Trim pastry to ½ inch from rim of pan; set aside.

❖ In large bowl combine all filling ingredients <u>except</u> apples, 1 tablespoon butter and 1 teaspoon sugar. Add apples; toss lightly to coat.

❖ Spoon apple mixture into prepared crust. Roll remaining pastry ball into 12-inch circle; cut 8 large slits in top crust. Place over pie; crimp or flute edge. Brush with melted 1 tablespoon butter; sprinkle with 1 teaspoon sugar. Cover edge of crust with 2-inch strip of aluminum foil.

❖ Bake for 35 minutes; remove aluminum foil. Continue baking for 10 to 20 minutes or until crust is lightly browned and juice begins to bubble through slits in crust. Cool pie 30 minutes; serve warm.

NUTRITION FACTS			
(1 SERVING)			
Calories	400	Fat	18g
Protein	4g	Cholesterol	25mg
Carbohydrate	60g	Sodium	170mg

TIP

If desired, remove pie from oven when lightly browned and bubbly. Run knife through slits in crust. Pour ½ cup whipping cream evenly through all slits. Return to oven for 5 minutes to warm whipping cream.

41

Easy Coconut Custard Pie

PREPARATION TIME: 10 minutes
BAKING TIME: 40 minutes

YIELD: 8 servings

2 cups milk
1 cup flaked coconut
¾ cup sugar
½ cup all-purpose flour
3 tablespoons LAND O LAKES® Butter, melted
4 eggs
1 teaspoon vanilla

Freshly grated whole nutmeg
Cut up fresh fruit

❖ Heat oven to 325°. In 5-cup blender container place milk; add all remaining ingredients <u>except</u> nutmeg and fruit. Cover; blend at medium speed until well mixed (1 to 2 minutes).

❖ Pour into greased and floured 9-inch pie pan; sprinkle with nutmeg. Bake for 40 to 45 minutes or until knife inserted in center comes out clean.

❖ Serve warm or chilled with fresh fruit. Store refrigerated.

NUTRITION FACTS (1 SERVING)			
Calories	250	Fat	11g
Protein	6g	Cholesterol	120mg
Carbohydrate	32g	Sodium	130mg

Frozen Strawberry Margarita Pie

PREPARATION TIME: 30 minutes   BAKING TIME: 8 minutes
CHILLING TIME: 45 minutes   FREEZING TIME: 6 hours   STANDING TIME: 20 minutes
YIELD: 8 servings

CRUST
1 cup finely crushed pretzels
3 tablespoons sugar
⅓ cup LAND O LAKES® Butter, melted

FILLING
2 (¼-ounce) envelopes unflavored gelatin
½ cup water
3 cups strawberries, hulled, <u>reserve 4</u>
½ cup sugar
¼ cup tequila <u>or</u> orange juice
1 cup strawberry lowfat yogurt
1 (6-ounce) can frozen limeade concentrate, slightly thawed

1 cup frozen whipped topping, thawed
8 small pretzels

❖ Heat oven to 350˚. In medium bowl stir together all crust ingredients. Press on bottom and up sides of 9-inch pie pan. Bake for 8 to 10 minutes or until lightly browned. Cool completely.

❖ Meanwhile, in small saucepan sprinkle gelatin over water; let stand 5 minutes to soften. Cook over medium heat until gelatin is dissolved (1 to 2 minutes).

❖ In food processor bowl or 5-cup blender container place strawberries. Cover; process on high speed until pureed (1 minute). Add gelatin mixture, sugar, tequila, yogurt and limeade. Process until well mixed. Cover; refrigerate until mixture mounds when dropped from spoon (45 to 60 minutes).

❖ Spoon into prepared crust. Freeze until firm (6 hours or overnight).

❖ Slice reserved strawberries. Garnish pie with strawberry slices, whipped topping and pretzels. Let stand at room temperature 20 to 30 minutes before serving.

NUTRITION FACTS (1 SERVING)			
Calories	280	Fat	8g
Protein	4g	Cholesterol	15mg
Carbohydrate	46g	Sodium	280mg

BREADS & COFFEE CAKES

*W*hether destined for family and friends or for the bake sale, a good coffee cake quickly disappears. For an encore, serve up a batch of piping hot muffins, scones or freshly baked bread spread with LAND O LAKES® Butter.

Country Rosemary Bread

PREPARATION TIME: 1 hour
RISING TIME: 1 hour 45 minutes   BAKING TIME: 20 minutes

Yield: 2 loaves (16 servings)

3   tablespoons
    LAND O LAKES®
    Butter
½   cup coarsely
    chopped onion
1   tablespoon
    chopped fresh
    rosemary*
2   teaspoons salt
½   teaspoon coarsely
    ground pepper
1   cup milk
1   (¼-ounce)
    package active
    dry yeast
1   cup warm water
    (105 to 115°F)
2   tablespoons
    sugar
½   cup yellow corn-
    meal
3½ to 4½ cups
    all-purpose flour

    All-purpose flour

* Substitute
  1 teaspoon dried
  rosemary, crushed.

◆ In 10-inch skillet melt butter until sizzling; add onion, rosemary, salt and pepper. Cook over medium heat, stirring occasionally, until onion is tender (5 to 7 minutes). Stir in milk. Cool to warm (105 to 115°F).

◆ In large bowl dissolve yeast in warm water; stir in sugar. Add warm butter mixture, cornmeal and 1 cup flour. Beat until smooth (1 to 2 minutes). Stir in enough remaining flour to make dough easy to handle.

◆ Turn dough onto lightly floured surface; knead until smooth and elastic (about 5 minutes). Place in greased bowl; turn greased side up. Cover; let rise in warm place until double in size (about 1 hour). Dough is ready if indentation remains when touched.

◆ Punch down dough; divide dough in half. Let stand 10 minutes. On lightly floured surface shape each half into 5-inch round loaf. Place on greased cookie sheet. Sprinkle with flour. Cover; let rise until double in size (about 45 minutes).

◆ Heat oven to 375°. With serrated knife make 3 diagonal slashes across top of each loaf; make 3 additional diagonal slashes in opposite direction. Bake for 20 to 25 minutes or until golden brown.

| NUTRITION FACTS | | | |
(1 SERVING)			
Calories	160	Fat	3g
Protein	4g	Cholesterol	5mg
Carbohydrate	27g	Sodium	300mg

CHEESE N' DILL SCONES

PREPARATION TIME: 30 minutes
BAKING TIME: 13 minutes

YIELD: 16 scones

2½ cups all-purpose flour

¼ cup chopped fresh parsley

1 tablespoon baking powder

2 teaspoons dried dill weed

½ teaspoon salt

¾ cup LAND O LAKES® Butter

5 ounces (1⅓ cups) LAND O LAKES® Cheddar Cheese, shredded

½ cup LAND O LAKES® Sour Cream (Regular, Light or No•Fat)

¼ cup milk

2 eggs, slightly beaten

❖ Heat oven to 400°. In medium bowl combine flour, parsley, baking powder, dill weed and salt; cut in butter until crumbly. Stir in 1 cup cheese. Stir in sour cream, milk and eggs just until moistened.

❖ Turn dough onto lightly floured surface; knead until smooth (1 minute). Divide dough in half; roll each half into 8-inch circle. Cut each circle into 8 wedges. Place 1 inch apart on cookie sheet.

❖ Sprinkle each with about 1 teaspoonful cheese. Bake for 13 to 18 minutes or until lightly browned. Serve warm.

NUTRITION FACTS (1 SCONE)			
Calories	210	Fat	14g
Protein	6g	Cholesterol	60mg
Carbohydrate	16g	Sodium	300mg

Jeweled Apricot Bread

Preparation time: 1 hour 15 minutes
Rising time: 2 hours Baking time: 25 minutes

Yield: 1 loaf (12 servings)

BREAD

⅓ cup sugar
½ cup LAND O LAKES® Butter
½ cup milk
¾ teaspoon salt
1 (¼-ounce) package active dry yeast
½ cup warm water (105 to 115°F)
3 to 4 cups all-purpose flour
1 egg
2 teaspoons grated lemon peel
½ teaspoon ground nutmeg

FILLING

½ cup sugar
1½ cups water
1 (6-ounce) package dried apricots
½ teaspoon ground nutmeg
2 tablespoons LAND O LAKES® Butter, softened
1 tablespoon LAND O LAKES® Butter, melted

GLAZE

¼ cup sugar
¼ cup LAND O LAKES® Sour Cream (Regular, Light or No•Fat)
2 tablespoons LAND O LAKES® Butter
2 teaspoons grated lemon peel

❖ In 1-quart saucepan combine ⅓ cup sugar, ½ cup butter, milk and salt. Cook over medium heat, stirring occasionally, until butter is melted (6 to 8 minutes). Cool to warm (105 to 115°F).

❖ In large mixer bowl dissolve yeast in ½ cup warm water. Add butter mixture, 2 cups flour, egg, 2 teaspoons lemon peel and ½ teaspoon nutmeg. Beat at medium speed, scraping bowl often, until smooth (1 to 2 minutes). By hand, stir in enough remaining flour to make dough easy to handle. Turn dough onto lightly floured surface; knead until smooth and elastic (about 5 minutes). Place in greased bowl; turn greased side up. Cover; let rise in warm place until double in size (about 1½ hours). Dough is ready if indentation remains when touched.

❖ Meanwhile, in 2-quart saucepan combine ½ cup sugar, 1½ cups water, apricots and ½ teaspoon nutmeg. Cook over medium heat until mixture comes to a full boil (3 to 5 minutes). Reduce heat to low. Cook, stirring occasionally, until apricots are tender and mixture is thickened (30 to 40 minutes); set aside.

❖ Punch down dough; let rest 10 minutes. On lightly floured surface roll dough into 15x10-inch rectangle. Spread dough with 2 tablespoons butter and apricot mixture to within ½ inch of edges. Roll up jelly-roll fashion beginning with 15-inch side. Place on large greased cookie sheet. Form into circle; pinch ends to seal. With serrated knife make cuts ⅔ of the way through dough every 1½ inches. Twist each section of dough, turning it on its side to form ring. Cover; let rise about 30 minutes.

❖ Heat oven to 350°. Bake for 25 to 35 minutes or until golden brown. Remove from pan; cool on wire rack. Brush with 1 tablespoon butter.

❖ Meanwhile, in 1-quart saucepan combine all glaze ingredients. Cook over medium heat, stirring occasionally, until mixture comes to a full boil (4 to 5 minutes). Cool 2 to 3 minutes. Pour warm glaze over bread. Store refrigerated.

NUTRITION FACTS
(1 SERVING)

Calories	350	Fat	14g
Protein	14g	Cholesterol	55mg
Carbohydrate	52g	Sodium	280mg

KATHRYN'S BLUEBERRY COFFEE CAKE

PREPARATION TIME: 20 minutes BAKING TIME: 40 minutes

YIELD: 12 servings

COFFEE CAKE

2¼ cups all-purpose flour
1¼ cups sugar
½ cup LAND O LAKES® Butter, softened
⅓ cup milk
2 eggs
1 (8-ounce) package cream cheese, softened
½ teaspoon baking soda
¼ teaspoon salt
1 teaspoon vanilla
1 cup fresh or frozen blueberries
2 tablespoons all-purpose flour

TOPPING

3 tablespoons LAND O LAKES® Butter
½ cup all-purpose flour
½ cup firmly packed brown sugar
1 teaspoon cinnamon

❖ Heat oven to 350°. In large mixer bowl combine all coffee cake ingredients <u>except</u> blueberries and 2 tablespoons flour. Beat at low speed, scraping bowl often, until well mixed (1 to 2 minutes).

❖ In medium bowl toss together blueberries and 2 tablespoons flour; gently stir into batter. Spoon into greased 13x9-inch baking pan.

❖ In 1-quart saucepan melt 3 tablespoons butter; stir in remaining topping ingredients. Sprinkle over batter. Bake for 40 to 55 minutes or until toothpick inserted in center comes out clean.

Marjorie's Almond Brickle Coffee Cake

PREPARATION TIME: 30 minutes BAKING TIME: 30 minutes COOLING TIME: 30 minutes

YIELD: 16 servings

COFFEE CAKE
1½ cups sugar
¾ cup LAND O LAKES® Butter, softened
4 eggs
1 teaspoon almond extract
1 teaspoon vanilla
3 cups all-purpose flour
1½ cups LAND O LAKES® Sour Cream (Regular, Light or No•Fat)
1½ teaspoons baking powder
1½ teaspoons baking soda
¼ teaspoon salt

STREUSEL
½ cup chopped dried apricots*
½ cup sliced almonds, toasted
½ cup almond brickle bits

GLAZE
½ cup powdered sugar
¼ teaspoon almond extract
2 to 3 teaspoons milk

* Substitute 1 (6-ounce) container fresh raspberries.

❖ Heat oven to 350°. In large mixer bowl combine sugar, butter, eggs, almond extract and vanilla. Beat at medium speed, scraping bowl often, until creamy (2 to 3 minutes). Add all remaining coffee cake ingredients. Continue beating, scraping bowl often, until well mixed (1 to 2 minutes).

❖ Spread ¼ of batter into each of 2 greased and floured 9-inch round cake pans. Sprinkle ¼ cup apricots over batter in each pan. Sprinkle 2 tablespoons almonds and 2 tablespoons almond brickle bits over apricots in each pan. Spread remaining batter over streusel filling in each pan; sprinkle with remaining almonds and almond brickle bits.

❖ Bake for 30 to 40 minutes or until toothpick inserted in center comes out clean. Cool 10 minutes; remove from pans. Cool completely.

❖ In small bowl stir together powdered sugar, almond extract and enough milk for desired glazing consistency. Drizzle over cooled coffee cakes.

CRANBERRY SOUR CREAM CRUMBLE

PREPARATION TIME: 30 minutes
BAKING TIME: 1 hour 10 minutes

YIELD: 12 servings

TOPPING

- ½ cup all-purpose flour
- ⅓ cup sugar
- ¼ cup chopped almonds
- ¼ cup LAND O LAKES® Butter, melted
- ¼ teaspoon vanilla

COFFEE CAKE

- ¼ cup chopped almonds
- 1 cup sugar
- ½ cup LAND O LAKES® Butter, softened
- 1 teaspoon vanilla
- 2 eggs
- 2 cups all-purpose flour
- 1¼ teaspoons baking powder
- ½ teaspoon baking soda
- ¼ teaspoon salt
- 1 cup LAND O LAKES® Sour Cream (Regular, Light or No•Fat)
- 1 cup whole cranberry sauce

❖ In medium bowl stir together all topping ingredients until crumbly; set aside.

❖ Heat oven to 350°. Sprinkle ¼ cup chopped almonds on bottom of greased 9-inch springform pan or 10-inch tube pan; set aside.

❖ In large mixer bowl combine 1 cup sugar, ½ cup butter and 1 teaspoon vanilla. Beat at medium speed, scraping bowl often, until creamy (1 to 2 minutes). Add eggs; continue beating, scraping bowl often, until well mixed (1 to 2 minutes). Continue beating, adding 2 cups flour, baking powder, baking soda and salt alternately with sour cream, until well mixed (1 to 2 minutes).

❖ Spoon half of batter into prepared pan; spread to cover bottom. Spread cranberry sauce over batter; spread to edges. Spread remaining batter over cranberry sauce to cover. Sprinkle topping over batter.

❖ Bake for 70 to 85 minutes or until toothpick inserted in center comes out clean. Cool 10 minutes; remove rim from springform pan.

NUTRITION FACTS			
(1 SERVING)			
Calories	390	Fat	18g
Protein	5g	Cholesterol	70mg
Carbohydrate	53g	Sodium	290mg

Orange Sugared Scones

PREPARATION TIME: 25 minutes
BAKING TIME: 25 minutes

YIELD: 1 dozen scones

2½ cups all-purpose flour

2 teaspoons baking powder

½ teaspoon baking soda

½ teaspoon salt

½ teaspoon cinnamon

½ cup LAND O LAKES® Butter, chilled

½ cup sugar

½ cup currants or raisins

1 tablespoon grated orange peel

1 cup LAND O LAKES® Sour Cream (Regular, Light or No•Fat)

1 egg, separated

4 teaspoons lemon juice

2 tablespoons sugar

❖ Heat oven to 375°. In large bowl combine flour, baking powder, baking soda, salt and cinnamon; cut in butter until crumbly.

❖ In small bowl combine ½ cup sugar, currants and orange peel. Stir into flour mixture.

❖ In medium bowl, with wire whisk, stir together sour cream, egg yolk and lemon juice until smooth. Stir sour cream mixture into flour mixture. (Mixture will be dry.) Knead about 5 to 8 times to combine all ingredients.

❖ Divide dough in half. Pat each half into 6-inch circle. Place both 6-inch circles on large greased cookie sheet. Cut each circle into 6 wedges.

❖ In small bowl beat egg white with fork until frothy. Brush tops of scones with egg white; sprinkle with 2 tablespoons sugar. Bake for 25 to 30 minutes or until scones are lightly browned. To serve, separate into individual scones.

NUTRITION FACTS (1 SCONE)			
Calories	240	Fat	10g
Protein	4g	Cholesterol	45mg
Carbohydrate	34g	Sodium	280mg

Prize-Winning Blueberry Muffins

PREPARATION TIME: 20 minutes BAKING TIME: 20 minutes

YIELD: 1 dozen muffins

½ cup sugar
¼ cup LAND O LAKES®
   Butter, softened
1 cup LAND O LAKES®
   Sour Cream
   (Regular, Light or
   No•Fat)
2 tablespoons
   lemon juice
1½ teaspoons grated
   lemon peel
1 egg
1½ cups all-purpose
   flour
1 teaspoon baking
   soda
1 cup fresh or
   frozen blueberries
   (unthawed)

1 tablespoon sugar
½ teaspoon grated
   lemon peel

❖Heat oven to 375°. In large mixer bowl combine ½ cup sugar and butter. Beat at medium speed, scraping bowl often, until creamy (1 to 2 minutes). Add sour cream, lemon juice, 1½ teaspoons lemon peel and egg. Continue beating, scraping bowl often, until well mixed (1 to 2 minutes).

❖In medium bowl stir together flour and baking soda. By hand, stir flour mixture into sour cream mixture just until moistened. Gently stir in blueberries. Spoon into greased or paper-lined 12-cup muffin pan.

❖In small bowl stir together 1 tablespoon sugar and ½ teaspoon lemon peel. Sprinkle about ¼ teaspoon mixture on top of each muffin. Bake for 20 to 25 minutes or until lightly browned. Cool 5 minutes; remove from pan.

NUTRITION FACTS			
(1 MUFFIN)			
Calories	170	Fat	6g
Protein	4g	Cholesterol	50mg
Carbohydrate	26g	Sodium	165mg

Sparkling Cranberry Muffins

PREPARATION TIME: 15 minutes BAKING TIME: 20 minutes

YIELD: 1 dozen muffins

FILLING
1 cup chopped fresh <u>or</u> frozen cranberries
2 tablespoons sugar

MUFFINS
2 cups all-purpose flour
⅓ cup sugar
2 teaspoons baking powder
½ teaspoon salt
½ cup LAND O LAKES® Butter
¾ cup orange juice
1 egg, slightly beaten

TOPPING
¼ cup LAND O LAKES® Butter, melted
¼ cup sugar

❖ Heat oven to 400°. In small bowl combine cranberries and 2 tablespoons sugar; set aside.

❖ In large bowl stir together flour, ⅓ cup sugar, baking powder and salt; cut in ½ cup butter until crumbly. Stir in orange juice and egg just until moistened. Gently stir in cranberry-sugar mixture.

❖ Spoon batter into greased or paper-lined 12-cup muffin pan. Bake for 20 to 25 minutes or until golden brown. Cool 5 minutes; remove from pan.

❖ For topping, dip top of each muffin in melted butter, then in sugar. Serve warm.

Tip
Divide batter between 2 greased 5½x3-inch mini loaf pans. Bake for 45 to 50 minutes or until toothpick inserted in center comes out clean. Cover loaves with aluminum foil while baking if browning too quickly.

NUTRITION FACTS (1 MUFFIN)			
Calories	240	Fat	12g
Protein	3g	Cholesterol	45mg
Carbohydrate	31g	Sodium	290mg

Almond Danish Kringle

PREPARATION TIME: 1 hour CHILLING TIME: 2 hours RISING TIME: 30 minutes
BAKING TIME: 13 minutes COOLING TIME: 30 minutes

YIELD: 2 kringles (16 servings)

KRINGLE
2¼ cups all-purpose flour
2 tablespoons sugar
½ teaspoon salt
½ cup LAND O LAKES® Butter
1 (¼-ounce) package active dry yeast
¼ cup warm water (105 to 115°F)
½ cup whipping cream
1 egg

FILLING
1 (7-ounce) package almond paste
¼ cup firmly packed brown sugar
¼ cup LAND O LAKES® Butter, softened

GLAZE
1 cup powdered sugar
1 tablespoon milk
½ teaspoon almond extract

Sliced almonds
Candied fruit

❖ In large bowl combine flour, 2 tablespoons sugar and salt; cut in butter until crumbly. Dissolve yeast in warm water. Stir yeast, whipping cream and egg into flour mixture. Cover; refrigerate until dough is firm (2 to 4 hours).

❖ In small mixer bowl combine all filling ingredients. Beat at medium speed, scraping bowl often, until well mixed (1 to 2 minutes); set aside.

❖ Divide dough in half. Return half to refrigerator. On lightly floured surface roll dough into 15x6-inch rectangle. Spread half of filling lengthwise down center of rectangle in 2-inch strip. Fold sides of dough over filling; pinch seam and ends to seal well. Place kringle, seam side down, on greased cookie sheet in horseshoe shape. Repeat with remaining dough. Cover; let rise about 30 minutes.

❖ Heat oven to 375°. Bake, 1 kringle at a time, for 13 to 23 minutes or until golden brown. Cool completely.

❖ In small bowl stir together all glaze ingredients. Spread over cooled kringles. Garnish with sliced almonds and candied fruit, if desired.

NUTRITION FACTS (1 SERVING)			
Calories	270	Fat	16g
Protein	4g	Cholesterol	50mg
Carbohydrate	30g	Sodium	165mg

Double Caramel-Raisin Rolls

PREPARATION TIME: 30 minutes
RISING TIME: 2 hours   BAKING TIME: 25 minutes

YIELD: 1½ dozen rolls

DOUGH
4½ to 5 cups all-pur-
    pose flour
⅓   cup sugar
1   cup warm milk
    (120 to 130°F)
½   cup LAND O LAKES®
    Butter, melted
1   (¼-ounce) package
    active dry yeast
2   eggs
½   teaspoon salt
¾   cup raisins

FILLING
1¼ cups firmly packed
    brown sugar
⅔   cup LAND O LAKES®
    Butter, melted
3   tablespoons light
    corn syrup
1½ teaspoons
    cinnamon

❖In large mixer bowl combine <u>2 cups</u> flour, sugar, warm milk, ½ cup butter, yeast, eggs and salt. Beat at medium speed, scraping bowl often, until smooth (1 to 2 minutes). By hand, stir in raisins and enough remaining flour to make dough easy to handle. Turn dough onto lightly floured surface; knead until smooth and elastic (3 to 5 minutes). Place in greased bowl; turn greased side up. Cover; let rise in warm place until double in size (about 1 to 1½ hours). Dough is ready if indentation remains when touched.

❖Punch down dough. In medium bowl stir together all filling ingredients <u>except</u> cinnamon. Spread <u>half</u> of filling on bottom of greased 13x9-inch baking pan. Stir cinnamon into remaining filling.

❖On lightly floured surface roll dough into 18x9-inch rectangle; spread with remaining filling. Roll up, jelly-roll fashion, beginning with 18-inch side. Pinch edge of dough into roll to seal well. Cut into 1-inch slices; place slices in prepared pan. Cover; let rise until double in size (about 1 hour).

❖<u>Heat oven to 375°.</u> Bake for 25 to 30 minutes or until golden brown. Immediately invert pan onto serving platter; remove pan.

TIP

Two (1-pound) loaves frozen bread dough can be substituted for dough recipe. Let frozen dough thaw according to package directions. Knead ¾ cup raisins into dough. Prepare filling and continue as directed above.

NUTRITION FACTS (1 ROLL)			
Calories	340	Fat	13g
Protein	5g	Cholesterol	55mg
Carbohydrate	51g	Sodium	200mg

Fresh Sage & Pepper Popovers

PREPARATION TIME: 30 minutes BAKING TIME: 40 minutes

YIELD: 6 popovers

POPOVERS
3 eggs
1¼ cups milk
1¼ cups all-purpose flour
1½ teaspoons chopped fresh
   sage leaves*
¼ teaspoon coarsely ground
   pepper
¼ teaspoon salt

SAGE BUTTER
½ cup LAND O LAKES® Butter,
   softened
1½ teaspoons fresh sage leaves*
¼ teaspoon coarsely ground
   pepper

* Substitute ½ teaspoon dried
sage leaves.

TIP
*Eggs and milk should be at
room temperature (72°F) to help
ensure successful popovers.*

❖Heat oven to 450°. In small
mixer bowl beat eggs at medium
speed, scraping bowl often, until
light yellow (1 to 2 minutes).
Add milk; continue beating
1 minute. By hand, stir in all
remaining popover ingredients.

❖Pour batter into greased 6-cup
popover pan or 6 (6-ounce)
custard cups. Bake for 15 minutes. Reduce oven temperature
to 350°. DO NOT OPEN OVEN
DOOR. Continue baking for 25
to 30 minutes or until golden
brown.

❖Meanwhile, in small mixer
bowl beat all sage butter ingredients at low speed, scraping
bowl often, until creamy (1 to 2
minutes).

❖Insert knife into popovers to
allow steam to escape. Serve
immediately with sage butter.

NUTRITION FACTS			
(1 POPOVER)			
Calories	300	Fat	19g
Protein	8g	Cholesterol	150mg
Carbohydrate	23g	Sodium	300mg

Raspberry Streusel Coffee Cake

Preparation time: 30 minutes
Baking time: 30 minutes

Yield: 9 servings

COFFEE CAKE

2 cups all-purpose flour
¾ cup sugar
½ cup milk
¼ cup Land O Lakes® Butter, softened
1 egg
2 teaspoons baking powder
½ teaspoon salt
½ teaspoon ground nutmeg
1 cup fresh or frozen raspberries (unthawed)

TOPPING

½ cup sugar
⅓ cup all-purpose flour
½ teaspoon cinnamon
½ teaspoon ground nutmeg
¼ cup Land O Lakes® Butter

❖ Heat oven to 375°. In large mixer bowl combine all coffee cake ingredients <u>except</u> raspberries. Beat at low speed until well mixed.

❖ By hand, gently stir in raspberries. Spread into greased and floured 9-inch square baking pan.

❖ In small bowl stir together all topping ingredients <u>except</u> butter; cut in butter until crumbly. Sprinkle over batter.

❖ Bake for 30 to 35 minutes or until toothpick inserted in center comes out clean.

NUTRITION FACTS			
(1 SERVING)			
Calories	340	Fat	12g
Protein	5g	Cholesterol	55mg
Carbohydrate	55g	Sodium	310mg

Golden Pumpkin Bread

PREPARATION TIME: 30 minutes
BAKING TIME: 45 minutes

YIELD: 3 loaves (24 servings)

1½ cups all-purpose flour
1 cup firmly packed brown sugar
1 cup canned pumpkin*
½ cup Land O Lakes® Butter, softened
2 eggs
1½ teaspoons cinnamon
1 teaspoon baking powder
1 teaspoon baking soda
1 teaspoon salt
½ teaspoon ground ginger
¼ teaspoon ground cloves

* Substitute 1 cup mashed cooked pumpkin.

✤ Heat oven to 350°. In large mixer bowl combine all ingredients. Beat at medium speed, scraping bowl often, until well mixed (2 to 3 minutes).

✤ Spoon into 3 greased 5½x3-inch mini loaf pans. Bake for 30 to 35 minutes or until toothpick inserted in center comes out clean. Cool 10 minutes; remove from pans. Cool completely; store refrigerated.

Tip

*Substitute 1 greased
9x5-inch loaf pan.
Bake for 45 to 55 minutes
or until toothpick inserted in
center comes out clean.*

NUTRITION FACTS			
(1 Serving)			
Calories	110	Fat	4g
Protein	1g	Cholesterol	30mg
Carbohydrate	16g	Sodium	200mg

Southwestern-Style Corn Bread

PREPARATION TIME: 15 minutes
BAKING TIME: 13 minutes

YIELD: 2 dozen

1¼ cups all-purpose flour
¾ cup yellow or blue cornmeal
3 tablespoons sugar
2 teaspoons baking powder
½ teaspoon salt
¼ cup LAND O LAKES® Butter, melted
1 cup milk
1 egg, slightly beaten
1 cup frozen whole kernel corn, thawed, drained
2 tablespoons chopped green chilies
2 tablespoons chopped green onion

❖ Heat oven to 400°. In large bowl combine flour, cornmeal, sugar, baking powder and salt. Stir in butter, milk and egg just until moistened. Gently stir in corn, chilies and onion.

❖ Fill greased corn bread stick pans almost full. Bake for 13 to 18 minutes or until very lightly browned. Cool 5 minutes; remove from pans. Serve warm.

TIP
To make corn bread, spoon batter into greased 9-inch square baking pan. Bake for 25 to 30 minutes or until lightly browned. 12 servings.

CAKES

*D*on't wait for a special occasion to bake one of these delicious cakes, many of which can be prepared with a minimum of fuss. Be sure to use real LAND O LAKES® Butter to ensure the best texture and flavor.

Chocolate Brownie Almond Bundt Cake

PREPARATION TIME: 15 minutes   BAKING TIME: 55 minutes
COOLING TIME: 1 hour   COOKING TIME: 2 minutes

YIELD: 16 servings

Tip

Use remaining half of boxes to make second cake.
Wrap unfrosted cake in plastic food wrap; freeze.
When ready to serve, let thaw. Prepare chocolate
ganache and drizzle over cake.

Cake

¼ cup unsweetened cocoa
1 (7.5-ounce) box chocolate fudge flavor dry icing mix
½ (18.25-ounce) box devil's food cake mix
½ (19.8 to 21.5-ounce) box brownie mix
1 cup LAND O LAKES® Sour Cream (Regular, Light or No•Fat)
⅔ cup half-and-half
½ cup chocolate-flavored syrup
3 eggs
2 teaspoons vanilla
2 teaspoons almond extract
⅔ cup chopped almonds, toasted

Chocolate Ganache

1 (6-ounce) package (1 cup) semi-sweet real chocolate chips
3 tablespoons LAND O LAKES® Butter
2 tablespoons half-and-half
1 tablespoon vegetable oil
1 teaspoon almond extract

❖ Heat oven to 350°. Generously spray 12-cup Bundt pan with no stick cooking spray; dust with ¼ cup unsweetened cocoa. Spray with no stick cooking spray again; set aside.

❖ In large mixer bowl combine all remaining cake ingredients except almonds. Beat at low speed, scraping bowl often, until well mixed (1 to 2 minutes). By hand, stir in almonds.

❖ Pour batter into prepared pan. Bake for 55 to 70 minutes or until cake begins to pull away from sides of pan. DO NOT OVERBAKE. Cool 10 minutes; invert onto serving platter. Cool completely.

❖ Meanwhile, in 1-quart saucepan combine all chocolate ganache ingredients except almond extract. Cook over low heat, stirring constantly, until chips are melted and consistency is pourable (2 to 3 minutes). Stir in 1 teaspoon almond extract. Drizzle over cooled cake.

NUTRITION FACTS (1 SERVING)			
Calories	390	Fat	20g
Protein	6g	Cholesterol	50mg
Carbohydrate	52g	Sodium	280mg

Cinnamon Almond Streusel Pound Cake

PREPARATION TIME: 25 minutes BAKING TIME: 45 minutes COOLING TIME: 15 minutes

YIELD: 16 servings

FILLING
⅓ cup firmly packed brown sugar
⅓ cup quick-cooking oats
1 teaspoon cinnamon
2 tablespoons LAND O LAKES® Butter
½ cup slivered almonds, coarsely chopped

CAKE
1 cup sugar
1 cup LAND O LAKES® Butter, softened
⅓ cup almond paste
5 eggs
1 teaspoon almond extract
1 teaspoon vanilla
1¼ cups all-purpose flour
1 cup cake flour*
1 teaspoon baking powder
¼ cup milk

GLAZE
1 cup powdered sugar
½ teaspoon almond extract
1 to 2 tablespoons milk
2 tablespoons sliced almonds

* Substitute 1 cup minus 2 tablespoons all-purpose flour.

❖ Heat oven to 350°. In small mixer bowl combine all filling ingredients. Beat at low speed until well mixed (1 minute); set aside.

❖ In large mixer bowl combine sugar, 1 cup butter and almond paste. Beat at medium speed, scraping bowl often, until creamy (1 to 2 minutes). Continue beating, adding eggs 1 at a time, until well mixed. Add almond extract and vanilla. Reduce speed to low. Beat, gradually adding flour, cake flour and baking powder alternately with milk and scraping bowl often, until well mixed (1 to 2 minutes).

❖ Pour <u>half</u> of batter into greased and floured 10-inch tube pan <u>or</u> 12-cup Bundt pan. Sprinkle filling over batter but not touching sides of pan. Spoon remaining batter over filling. Bake for 45 to 55 minutes or until toothpick inserted in center comes out clean. Cool 15 minutes; remove from pan.

❖ Meanwhile, in small bowl combine powdered sugar, almond extract and enough milk for desired glazing consistency. Drizzle over warm cake; sprinkle with sliced almonds.

NUTRITION FACTS (1 SERVING)			
Calories	350	Fat	19g
Protein	6g	Cholesterol	100mg
Carbohydrate	41g	Sodium	180mg

Rocky Road Chocolate Cake

PREPARATION TIME: 20 minutes
BAKING TIME: 32 minutes

YIELD: 15 servings

CAKE

2 cups all-purpose flour
1½ cups sugar
½ cup unsweetened cocoa
½ cup LAND O LAKES® Butter, softened
1 cup water
3 eggs
1¼ teaspoons baking powder
1 teaspoon baking soda
1 teaspoon vanilla

FROSTING

2 cups miniature marshmallows
¼ cup LAND O LAKES® Butter
1 (3-ounce) package cream cheese
1 (1-ounce) square unsweetened chocolate
2 tablespoons milk
3 cups powdered sugar
1 teaspoon vanilla
½ cup coarsely chopped salted peanuts

❖ Heat oven to 350°. In large mixer bowl combine all cake ingredients. Beat at low speed, scraping bowl often, until all ingredients are moistened. Increase speed to high. Beat, scraping bowl often, until smooth (1 to 2 minutes).

❖ Pour batter into greased and floured 13x9-inch baking pan. Bake for 30 to 40 minutes or until toothpick inserted in center comes out clean. Sprinkle with marshmallows. Continue baking 2 minutes or until marshmallows are softened.

❖ Meanwhile, in 2-quart saucepan combine ¼ cup butter, cream cheese, chocolate and milk. Cook over medium heat, stirring occasionally, until melted (8 to 10 minutes). Remove from heat; stir in powdered sugar and vanilla until smooth. Pour over marshmallows and swirl together. Sprinkle with peanuts.

NUTRITION FACTS (1 SERVING)			
Calories	400	Fat	16g
Protein	6g	Cholesterol	75mg
Carbohydrate	61g	Sodium	290mg

CHOCOLATE SPONGE CAKE WITH FRESH FRUIT

PREPARATION TIME: 45 minutes   BAKING TIME: 20 minutes   COOLING TIME: 30 minutes

YIELD: 12 servings

CAKE

1 cup powdered sugar
4 eggs, room temperature
1 egg yolk, room temperature
1 tablespoon creme de cacao*
½ cup all-purpose flour
¼ cup Dutch process cocoa <u>or</u> unsweetened cocoa
⅛ teaspoon salt
2 tablespoons LAND O LAKES® Butter, melted

TOPPING

1 pint strawberries, hulled, cut in half
1 kiwi fruit, peeled, sliced ⅛ inch, cut in half
½ cup fresh blueberries
½ cup fresh raspberries
1 (10-ounce) jar apple jelly, melted

* Substitute 1 teaspoon vanilla.

❖ Heat oven to 375°. Grease and flour 10-inch tart pan with removable bottom. Place pan on cookie sheet; set aside.

❖ In large mixer bowl combine powdered sugar, eggs, egg yolk and creme de cacao. Beat at high speed, scraping bowl often, until mixture is very thick and double in volume (5 to 8 minutes). (Mixture should be light yellow and consistency of soft whipped cream.)

❖ In medium bowl stir together flour, cocoa and salt. By hand, gently stir flour mixture into egg mixture, ¼ cup at a time, just until flour mixture disappears. Gently stir melted butter into batter.

❖ Gently spoon batter into prepared pan. Bake for 20 to 23 minutes or until toothpick inserted in center comes out clean. Cool completely.

❖ To serve, decoratively arrange fresh fruit on top of cake. Drizzle melted jelly over top of cake and fruit.

NUTRITION FACTS (1 SERVING)			
Calories	190	Fat	5g
Protein	4g	Cholesterol	95mg
Carbohydrate	35g	Sodium	80mg

Chocolate Chip Banana Snack Cake

PREPARATION TIME: 30 minutes   BAKING TIME: 50 minutes

YIELD: 15 servings

3½ cups all-purpose flour
1 teaspoon baking powder
1 teaspoon baking soda
¼ teaspoon salt
2 cups sugar
½ cup LAND O LAKES® Butter, softened
2 eggs
2 medium (1 cup) ripe bananas, mashed
1 cup LAND O LAKES® Sour Cream (Regular, Light or No•Fat)
1 teaspoon vanilla
1½ cups miniature semi-sweet chocolate chips

❖Heat oven to 350°. In medium bowl stir together flour, baking powder, baking soda and salt; set aside.

❖In large mixer bowl combine sugar and butter. Beat at medium speed, scraping bowl often, until creamy (2 to 3 minutes). Continue beating, adding eggs one at a time, until well beaten (1 to 2 minutes). Add bananas, sour cream and vanilla; continue beating until well mixed (1 minute). Continue beating, gradually adding flour mixture and scraping bowl often, until well mixed (1 minute). By hand, gently stir in 1 cup chocolate chips.

❖Pour batter into greased 13x9-inch baking pan. Sprinkle remaining chocolate chips over batter. Bake for 40 to 50 minutes or until toothpick inserted in center comes out clean.

NUTRITION FACTS			
(1 SERVING)			
Calories	390	Fat	14g
Protein	5g	Cholesterol	50mg
Carbohydrate	64g	Sodium	210mg

Carrot Cake with Cream Cheese Frosting

PREPARATION TIME: 25 minutes   BAKING TIME: 40 minutes   COOLING TIME: 1 hour

YIELD: 15 servings

CAKE

1 cup firmly packed brown sugar
¾ cup sugar
1 cup LAND O LAKES® Butter, melted
3 eggs
1 (11-ounce) can mandarin oranges, undrained
2½ teaspoons vanilla
2 teaspoons grated orange peel
2¾ cups all-purpose flour
2 teaspoons baking soda
½ teaspoon salt
1 tablespoon cinnamon
¾ cup flaked coconut
½ cup chopped walnuts
4 medium (2 cups) carrots, grated

FROSTING

3½ cups powdered sugar
1 (8-ounce) package cream cheese, softened
2 tablespoons LAND O LAKES® Butter, softened
2 teaspoons vanilla

❖Heat oven to 350°. In large mixer bowl combine brown sugar, sugar, 1 cup butter and eggs. Beat at medium speed, scraping bowl often, until creamy (1 to 2 minutes). Add mandarin oranges, 2½ teaspoons vanilla and orange peel. Continue beating until well mixed (1 minute). Reduce speed to low; add flour, baking soda, salt and cinnamon. Beat, scraping bowl often, until creamy (1 to 2 minutes). By hand, stir in coconut, ½ cup walnuts and carrots.

❖Pour batter into greased and floured 13x9-inch baking pan. Bake for 40 to 50 minutes or until toothpick inserted in center comes out clean. Cool completely.

❖Meanwhile, in small mixer bowl combine all frosting ingredients. Beat at medium speed, scraping bowl often, until smooth. Frost cooled cake. Sprinkle with additional chopped walnuts, if desired.

NUTRITION FACTS			
(1 SERVING)			
Calories	520	Fat	24g
Protein	6g	Cholesterol	100mg
Carbohydrate	72g	Sodium	440mg

Pumpkin Pecan Layer Cake

PREPARATION TIME: 30 minutes
BAKING TIME: 25 minutes   COOLING TIME: 30 minutes

YIELD: 16 servings

TIP

To remove cake easily from pan, place wire cooling rack on top of cake and invert; repeat with remaining layers.

CAKE

2 cups crushed vanilla wafers
1 cup chopped pecans
½ cup LAND O LAKES® Butter, melted

1 (18-ounce) package carrot cake mix
1 cup pumpkin
¼ cup LAND O LAKES® Butter, melted
3 eggs
2 tablespoons water

FILLING

3 cups powdered sugar
⅔ cup LAND O LAKES® Butter, softened
4 ounces cream cheese, softened
2 teaspoons vanilla
¼ cup caramel topping

1 cup pecan halves

❖ Heat oven to 350°. In large mixer bowl combine wafer crumbs, chopped pecans and ½ cup melted butter until crumbly. Press mixture evenly and firmly on bottom of 3 greased and floured 8 or 9-inch round cake pans.

❖ In same bowl combine cake mix, pumpkin, ¼ cup melted butter, eggs and water. Beat at medium speed, scraping bowl often, until well mixed (2 to 3 minutes). Spread about 1½ cups batter over crumbs in each pan. Bake for 25 to 30 minutes or until toothpick inserted in center comes out clean. Cool 5 minutes; remove from pans. Cool completely.

❖ In small mixer bowl combine powdered sugar, ⅔ cup butter, cream cheese and vanilla. Beat at medium speed, scraping bowl often, until smooth. On serving plate layer 3 cake layers, nut side down, with ½ cup filling spread between each layer. With remaining filling, frost sides only of cake. Spread caramel topping over top of cake, drizzling some over frosted sides. Arrange pecan halves in rings on top of cake. Store refrigerated.

NUTRITION FACTS (1 SERVING)			
Calories	570	Fat	34g
Protein	5g	Cholesterol	95mg
Carbohydrate	65g	Sodium	450mg

Lemon Picnic Cake with Berries

PREPARATION TIME: 30 minutes   BAKING TIME: 50 minutes
COOLING TIME: 15 minutes

YIELD: 16 servings

CAKE

4   eggs, separated
2   cups sugar
1   cup LAND O LAKES® Butter, softened
3   cups all-purpose flour
2   teaspoons baking powder
1   cup milk
2   teaspoons grated lemon peel
1   tablespoon lemon juice
1   teaspoon vanilla

GLAZE

⅓   cup sugar
⅓   cup lemon juice
1   tablespoon grated lemon peel

Fresh berries

❖ Heat oven to 350°. In small mixer bowl beat egg whites at high speed, scraping bowl often, just until stiff peaks form (2 to 3 minutes). Set aside.

❖ In large mixer bowl combine 2 cups sugar and butter. Beat at medium speed, scraping bowl often, until creamy (1 to 2 minutes). Add egg yolks; continue beating until creamy (1 to 2 minutes).

❖ In small bowl stir together flour and baking powder. Reduce speed to low. Beat, gradually adding flour mixture alternately with milk to butter mixture, until well blended. Add lemon peel, lemon juice and vanilla. Continue beating until well mixed. By hand, gently stir in egg whites.

❖ Pour batter into greased and floured 12-cup Bundt pan or 10-inch tube pan. Bake for 50 to 65 minutes or until toothpick inserted in center comes out clean.

❖ In 1-quart saucepan stir together all glaze ingredients <u>except</u> berries. Cook over medium heat, stirring occasionally, until sugar is dissolved (3 to 4 minutes). With toothpick, poke holes in top of cake; pour glaze over cake. Cool 15 minutes; remove from pan. Serve with fresh berries.

NUTRITION FACTS			
(1 SERVING)			
Calories	330	Fat	14g
Protein	5g	Cholesterol	85mg
Carbohydrate	49g	Sodium	180mg

Apple Crisp Cake with Rum Sauce

PREPARATION TIME: 45 minutes
BAKING TIME: 35 minutes

YIELD: 9 servings (1 cup sauce)

TOPPING
- ⅓ cup all-purpose flour
- ⅓ cup quick-cooking oats
- ¼ cup firmly packed brown sugar
- ¼ cup LAND O LAKES® Butter, softened

CAKE
- 1 cup all-purpose flour
- ½ cup sugar
- ½ cup LAND O LAKES® Sour Cream (Regular, Light or No•Fat)
- ¼ cup LAND O LAKES® Butter, softened
- 1 egg
- 1 teaspoon cinnamon
- ½ teaspoon baking powder
- ½ teaspoon baking soda
- ¼ teaspoon salt
- ½ cup chopped pecans
- 2 medium (2 cups) tart cooking apples, peeled, sliced ⅛ inch, cut in half

SAUCE
- ⅓ cup sugar
- ⅓ cup firmly packed brown sugar
- ¼ cup LAND O LAKES® Butter
- ¼ cup light corn syrup
- ⅓ cup whipping cream
- ½ teaspoon rum extract

❖ Heat oven to 375˚. In small mixer bowl combine all topping ingredients. Beat at low speed, until crumbly (1 to 2 minutes); set aside.

❖ In large mixer bowl combine all cake ingredients <u>except</u> pecans and apples. Beat at medium speed, scraping bowl often, until well mixed (2 to 3 minutes). By hand, stir in pecans. Spread batter into greased 9-inch square baking pan. Arrange apple slices in rows on top of batter. Sprinkle with reserved topping. Bake for 35 to 40 minutes or until topping is golden brown and apples are fork tender.

❖ Meanwhile, in 1-quart saucepan combine all sauce ingredients <u>except</u> whipping cream and rum extract. Cook over medium heat, stirring occasionally, until mixture comes to a full boil (6 to 10 minutes). Cool 5 minutes. Stir in ⅓ cup whipping cream and rum extract. Serve warm rum sauce over cake.

NUTRITION FACTS (1 SERVING)			
Calories	480	Fat	25g
Protein	5g	Cholesterol	80mg
Carbohydrate	62g	Sodium	330mg

Apricot Pecan Upside-Down Cake

PREPARATION TIME: 30 minutes
BAKING TIME: 30 minutes

YIELD: 9 servings

TOPPING

½ cup firmly packed brown sugar
¼ cup LAND O LAKES® Butter
¼ teaspoon ground nutmeg
½ cup chopped pecans
1 (16-ounce) can apricot halves, well drained

CAKE

⅔ cup firmly packed brown sugar
⅓ cup LAND O LAKES® Butter, softened
2 eggs
¾ teaspoon grated lemon peel
1½ teaspoons vanilla
1½ cups all-purpose flour
2 teaspoons baking powder
¼ teaspoon salt
½ cup milk

❖ Heat oven to 375°. Cut piece of waxed paper to fit bottom of 9-inch square or 11x7-inch baking pan; place on bottom.

❖ In small bowl combine all topping ingredients except pecans and apricots. Stir in pecans. Sprinkle on top of waxed paper. Place apricot halves, rounded side down, on top of brown sugar mixture; set aside.

❖ In large mixer bowl combine ⅔ cup brown sugar and ⅓ cup butter. Beat at medium speed, scraping bowl often, until creamy (1 to 2 minutes). Continue beating, adding eggs 1 at a time, until well mixed (1 to 2 minutes). Add lemon peel and vanilla; continue beating until well mixed (1 minute). Reduce speed to low. Beat, gradually adding flour, baking powder and salt alternately with milk and scraping bowl often, until well mixed (1 to 2 minutes). Gently spread batter on top of apricots.

❖ Bake for 30 to 40 minutes or until toothpick inserted in center comes out clean. Loosen sides of cake from pan by running a knife around inside of pan. Invert cake onto serving platter; let stand 5 minutes. Remove pan. Gently peel off waxed paper; cool completely.

NUTRITION FACTS (1 SERVING)			
Calories	370	Fat	18g
Protein	5g	Cholesterol	80mg
Carbohydrate	49g	Sodium	280mg

Lemon Poppy Seed Pound Cake

Preparation time: 30 minutes
Baking time: 55 minutes   Cooling time: 1 hour 30 minutes

Yield: 16 servings

CAKE
3 cups all-purpose flour
2 cups sugar
¼ cup poppy seeds
1 cup LAND O LAKES® Butter, softened
1 cup buttermilk
4 eggs
½ teaspoon baking powder
½ teaspoon baking soda
½ teaspoon salt
4 teaspoons grated lemon peel
½ teaspoon vanilla

GLAZE
1 cup powdered sugar
1 to 2 tablespoons lemon juice

❖Heat oven to 325°. In large mixer bowl combine all cake ingredients. Beat at low speed, scraping bowl often, until all ingredients are just moistened.

❖Increase speed to high. Beat, scraping bowl often, until well mixed (1 to 2 minutes).

❖Pour batter into greased and floured 12-cup Bundt pan <u>or</u> 10-inch tube pan. Bake for 55 to 65 minutes or until toothpick inserted in center comes out clean. Cool 10 minutes; remove from pan. Cool completely.

❖In small bowl stir together powdered sugar and enough lemon juice for glazing consistency; drizzle over cooled cake.

Tip
If you don't have 1 cup buttermilk,
measure and combine
1 tablespoon vinegar plus enough
milk to equal 1 cup.

NUTRITION FACTS			
(1 SERVING)			
Calories	340	Fat	14g
Protein	5g	Cholesterol	85mg
Carbohydrate	51g	Sodium	260mg

71

Buttery Coconut Pecan Cake

PREPARATION TIME: 30 minutes
BAKING TIME: 45 minutes   COOLING TIME: 1 hour

YIELD: 15 servings

CAKE

2¼ cups all-purpose flour
1½ cups sugar
1 cup LAND O LAKES® Butter, softened
1 cup buttermilk*
4 eggs
1 teaspoon baking soda
½ teaspoon salt
1 tablespoon vanilla
1 cup flaked coconut
1 cup chopped pecans

FROSTING

⅓ cup LAND O LAKES® Butter, melted
3 cups powdered sugar
1½ teaspoons vanilla
1 to 3 tablespoons milk

* Substitute 1 tablespoon vinegar plus enough milk to equal 1 cup.

❖ Heat oven to 350°. In large mixer bowl combine all cake ingredients <u>except</u> coconut and pecans. Beat at low speed, scraping bowl often, until all ingredients are moistened (1 to 2 minutes). Increase speed to high. Beat, scraping bowl often, until smooth (3 to 4 minutes). By hand, stir in coconut and pecans.

❖ Pour batter into greased and floured 13x9-inch baking pan. Bake for 45 to 50 minutes or until center of cake is firm to the touch and edges begin to pull away from sides of pan. Cool completely.

❖ In 1-quart saucepan heat ⅓ cup butter over medium heat, stirring constantly, until lightly browned (5 to 6 minutes).

❖ In small mixer bowl combine melted butter, powdered sugar and vanilla. Beat at medium speed, gradually adding milk and scraping bowl often, until smooth. Frost cooled cake.

NUTRITION FACTS			
(1 Serving)			
Calories	480	Fat	25g
Protein	5g	Cholesterol	100mg
Carbohydrate	63g	Sodium	350mg

Choco-Scotch Cake

PREPARATION TIME: 20 minutes
BAKING TIME: 40 minutes

YIELD: 15 servings

2½ cups all-purpose flour
1½ cups sugar
¾ cup LAND O LAKES® Butter, softened
1¼ cups cold water
3 eggs
2 (1-ounce) squares unsweetened baking chocolate, melted
1 teaspoon baking soda
1 teaspoon salt
1 teaspoon vanilla
1 cup butterscotch-flavored chips
½ cup chopped walnuts

❖Heat oven to 350°. In large mixer bowl combine all ingredients <u>except</u> butterscotch chips and walnuts. Beat at low speed, scraping bowl often, until all ingredients are moistened (1 to 2 minutes). Increase speed to medium. Beat, scraping bowl often, until well mixed (2 minutes).

❖Spread batter into greased 13x9-inch baking pan. Sprinkle with butterscotch chips and walnuts. Bake for 40 to 45 minutes or until top springs back when touched lightly in center. Cool completely.

NUTRITION FACTS
(1 SERVING)

Calories	350	Fat	19g
Protein	5g	Cholesterol	65mg
Carbohydrate	45g	Sodium	330mg

Tip

Substitute two 8-inch square baking pans for 13x9-inch pan. Bake as directed above.

Gingerbread Wedges with Cider Sauce

PREPARATION TIME: 20 minutes   BAKING TIME: 30 minutes

YIELD: 9 servings (1 cup sauce)

GINGERBREAD
1¾ cups all-purpose flour
⅓ cup firmly packed brown sugar
½ cup LAND O LAKES® Butter, softened
½ cup light molasses
½ cup buttermilk*
1 egg
1 teaspoon baking soda
½ teaspoon ground ginger
¼ teaspoon ground cloves
¼ teaspoon ground nutmeg

CIDER SAUCE
1 cup apple cider
⅓ cup firmly packed brown sugar
1 tablespoon LAND O LAKES® Butter
1 tablespoon lemon juice
Dash ground cloves
1 tablespoon cornstarch
1 tablespoon water

* Substitute 1½ teaspoons vinegar plus enough milk to equal ½ cup.

❖Heat oven to 350°. In large mixer bowl combine all gingerbread ingredients. Beat at low speed, scraping bowl often, until well mixed (2 to 3 minutes).

❖Pour batter into greased and floured 9-inch round cake pan. Bake for 30 to 40 minutes or until top springs back when touched lightly in center. Cool 10 minutes. Remove from pan.

❖Meanwhile, in 1-quart saucepan combine all cider sauce ingredients <u>except</u> cornstarch and water. Cook over medium heat, stirring occasionally, until mixture comes to a full boil (7 to 10 minutes). Boil 3 minutes.

❖In small bowl combine cornstarch and water. Stir into hot cider mixture. Continue cooking, stirring constantly, until sauce is thickened (1 to 2 minutes). Serve warm over gingerbread.

NUTRITION FACTS
(1 SERVING)

Calories	320	Fat	13g
Protein	4g	Cholesterol	55mg
Carbohydrate	50g	Sodium	410mg

HOLIDAY FRUITED POUND CAKE

PREPARATION TIME: 25 minutes
BAKING TIME: 1 hour   COOLING TIME: 1 hour 30 minutes

YIELD: 16 servings

CAKE

1½ cups sugar
1   cup LAND O LAKES® Butter, softened
4   ounces cream cheese, softened
6   eggs
1   tablespoon grated orange peel
1   tablespoon vanilla
1   teaspoon brandy extract
1   teaspoon rum extract
3   cups all-purpose flour
½   teaspoon baking powder
½   cup green candied cherries, coarsely chopped
½   cup red candied cherries, coarsely chopped
½   cup raisins

GLAZE

¾   cup powdered sugar
½   teaspoon rum extract
3 to 4 teaspoons milk

❖ Heat oven to 350°. In large mixer bowl combine sugar, butter and cream cheese. Beat at medium speed, scraping bowl often, until creamy (2 to 3 minutes). Add eggs, orange peel, vanilla, brandy extract and 1 teaspoon rum extract. Continue beating, scraping bowl often, until well mixed (2 to 3 minutes). Reduce speed to low; add flour and baking powder. Beat, scraping bowl often, until well mixed (2 to 3 minutes). By hand, stir in cherries and raisins.

❖ Spoon batter into greased and floured 12-cup Bundt pan or 10-inch tube pan. Bake for 60 to 70 minutes or until toothpick inserted in center comes out clean. Cool 10 minutes; remove from pan. Cool completely.

❖ In small bowl combine powdered sugar, ½ teaspoon rum extract and enough milk for desired glazing consistency. Drizzle over cooled cake. Garnish with green and red candied cherries, if desired.

NUTRITION FACTS (1 SERVING)			
Calories	390	Fat	16g
Protein	5g	Cholesterol	110mg
Carbohydrate	59g	Sodium	220mg

Grandma's Lazy Day Cake

PREPARATION TIME: 15 minutes
BAKING TIME: 25 minutes BROILING TIME: 2 minutes

YIELD: 15 servings

CAKE

½ cup LAND O LAKES® Butter

⅓ cup whipping cream

1¼ cups sugar

3 eggs

2 cups all-purpose flour

2 teaspoons baking powder

½ teaspoon salt

FROSTING

1 cup firmly packed brown sugar

1 cup chopped pecans

⅓ cup LAND O LAKES® Butter, melted

¼ cup whipping cream <u>or</u> milk

❖ Heat oven to 350°. In 1-quart saucepan combine ½ cup butter and ⅓ cup whipping cream. Cook over low heat, stirring occasionally, until butter melts (7 to 8 minutes); set aside.

❖ In large mixer bowl combine sugar and eggs. Beat at medium speed, scraping bowl often, until creamy (1 to 2 minutes). Add butter mixture, flour, baking powder and salt. Continue beating, scraping bowl often, until well mixed (1 to 2 minutes). Spread batter into greased and floured 13x9-inch baking pan. Bake for 25 to 30 minutes or until toothpick inserted in center comes out clean.

❖ Heat broiler. In small bowl stir together all frosting ingredients until well mixed. Spread over warm cake. Broil 2 to 4 inches from heat until bubbly (2 to 4 minutes). Serve warm or cool.

NUTRITION FACTS			
(1 SERVING)			
Calories	370	Fat	20g
Protein	4g	Cholesterol	85mg
Carbohydrate	46g	Sodium	240mg

DESSERTS

*S*elect
a treat from a wide array of
unforgettable desserts and
candies: Cobblers, toffees,
puddings, caramels and fudge
are some of the confections that
will bring a smile to
someone special. Blend in the
creamy goodness of sour cream
or butter from
LAND O'LAKES for the
best results.

Old-Fashioned Bread Pudding with Vanilla Sauce

Preparation time: 10 minutes Baking time: 40 minutes Cooking time: 5 minutes

Yield: 8 servings (1½ cups sauce)

Pudding

4	cups (8 slices) cubed white bread
½	cup raisins
2	cups milk
¼	cup LAND O LAKES® Butter
½	cup sugar
2	eggs, slightly beaten
½	teaspoon ground nutmeg
1	teaspoon vanilla

Sauce

½	cup sugar
½	cup firmly packed brown sugar
½	cup LAND O LAKES® Butter
½	cup whipping cream
1	teaspoon vanilla

❖ Heat oven to 350°. In large bowl combine bread and raisins. In 1-quart saucepan combine milk and ¼ cup butter. Cook over medium heat until butter is melted (4 to 7 minutes). Pour milk mixture over bread and raisin mixture; let stand 10 minutes.

❖ Stir in all remaining pudding ingredients. Pour into greased 1½-quart casserole. Bake for 40 to 50 minutes or until set in center.

❖ In 1-quart saucepan combine all sauce ingredients <u>except</u> vanilla. Cook over medium heat, stirring occasionally, until mixture thickens and comes to a full boil (5 to 8 minutes). Stir in vanilla.

❖ To serve, spoon warm pudding into individual dessert dishes; spoon sauce over. Store refrigerated.

PRALINE PECAN CREPES

PREPARATION TIME: 1 hour
COOKING TIME: 13 minutes

YIELD: 6 servings (2 cups sauce)

CREPES

¾ cup all-purpose flour
1½ teaspoons sugar
¼ teaspoon baking powder
¼ teaspoon salt
1 cup milk
1 egg
1 tablespoon LAND O LAKES® Butter, melted
¼ teaspoon vanilla
1 teaspoon LAND O LAKES® Butter

SAUCE

¼ cup LAND O LAKES® Butter
¼ cup sugar
¼ cup firmly packed brown sugar
1 tablespoon cornstarch
¼ cup chopped pecans
1¾ cups water
1 tablespoon vanilla

❖In small mixer bowl combine flour, 1½ teaspoons sugar, baking powder and salt. Add all remaining ingredients except 1 teaspoon butter. Beat at medium speed, scraping bowl often, until smooth (1 to 2 minutes).

❖Melt 1 teaspoon butter in 6 or 8-inch skillet until sizzling. For each of 6 crepes, pour about ¼ cup batter into skillet; immediately rotate skillet until thin film covers bottom. Cook over medium heat until lightly browned (2 to 3 minutes). Run wide spatula around edge to loosen; turn. Continue cooking until lightly browned (2 to 3 minutes). Place crepes on plate, placing waxed paper between each. Cover crepes; set aside.

❖In 10-inch skillet melt ¼ cup butter over medium heat; stir in ¼ cup sugar, brown sugar and cornstarch. Stir in all remaining sauce ingredients. Cook over medium heat, stirring occasionally, until sauce begins to thicken (5 to 6 minutes).

❖Meanwhile, fold each crepe in half; fold in half again to form triangles. When sauce begins to thicken arrange crepes in skillet. Cook, spooning sauce over crepes occasionally, until crepes are heated through (3 to 4 minutes). Serve warm crepes with sauce.

PUFF PASTRY STRAWBERRY LEMON TART

PREPARATION TIME: 1 hour BAKING TIME: 15 minutes
COOLING TIME: 15 minutes CHILLING TIME: 2 hours 15 minutes

YIELD: 8 servings

PASTRY

½ (17¼-ounce) package (2 sheets) frozen puff pastry sheets, thawed
1 egg yolk, slightly beaten

FILLING

⅔ cup sugar
½ cup LAND O LAKES® Butter
¼ cup lemon juice
3 egg yolks
1 tablespoon cornstarch
1 tablespoon grated lemon peel

GARNISH

1 pint strawberries, hulled, cut in half
Sweetened whipped cream

❖On lightly floured surface roll out pastry into 14x9-inch rectangle. Cut out 8-inch circle from dough. Using 2-inch round cookie cutter cut 6 circles from remaining dough. Cut 2-inch circles in half. Sprinkle cookie sheet with cold water; place 8-inch circle on cookie sheet. Brush pastry with beaten egg yolk; prick dough with fork. Place half-circles around outside edge of pastry. Brush with remaining egg yolk. Refrigerate 15 minutes.

❖Heat oven to 425°. Bake for 15 to 17 minutes or until golden brown. Cool completely.

❖In 2-quart saucepan combine all filling ingredients. Cook over medium heat, stirring constantly, until mixture comes to a full boil (5 to 6 minutes). Boil 1 minute. Cover surface with plastic food wrap; cool to room temperature. Pour filling into pastry; refrigerate until firm (2 to 3 hours).

❖To serve, arrange strawberries on top of filling and garnish with sweetened whipped cream.

Chocolate Caramel Truffle Torte

PREPARATION TIME: 45 minutes BAKING TIME: 15 minutes
COOLING TIME: 30 minutes CHILLING TIME: 2 hours

YIELD: 16 servings

CRUST
1¾ cups very finely
   chopped pecans
⅔ cup sugar
¼ cup LAND O LAKES®
   Butter, melted

FILLING
2 cups (1 pint)
   whipping cream
16 ounces high qual-
   ity semi-sweet
   real chocolate,
   coarsely
   chopped*

CARAMEL SAUCE
¾ cup firmly packed
   brown sugar
¾ cup sugar
½ cup light corn
   syrup
⅓ cup LAND O LAKES®
   Butter
⅔ cup whipping
   cream

GARNISH
1⅓ cups whipping
   cream

*Substitute 16
 ounces (2⅔ cups)
 semi-sweet real
 chocolate chips.

TIP

*Crust, filling and caramel sauce
can be prepared 1 day before
serving. Reheat caramel sauce just
before serving.*

❖Heat oven to 350°. In medium bowl stir together all crust ingredients. Firmly press on bottom and up sides of 12-inch tart pan with removable bottom. Place on cookie sheet. Bake for 15 to 18 minutes or until lightly browned. Cool completely.

❖In 2-quart saucepan place 2 cups whipping cream. Cook over medium heat until whipping cream just comes to a boil (5 to 8 minutes). Remove from heat; stir in chocolate until completely melted (2 to 3 minutes). Pour into cooled crust. Refrigerate until set (at least 2 hours).

❖Twenty minutes before serving, in 2-quart saucepan combine all caramel sauce ingredients <u>except</u> ⅔ cup whipping cream. Cook over medium heat, stirring occasionally, until mixture comes to a full boil (5 to 8 minutes). Cool 5 minutes; stir in ⅔ cup whipping cream.

❖Just before serving, in chilled small mixer bowl beat 1⅓ cups chilled whipping cream at high speed, scraping bowl often, until stiff peaks form (1 to 2 minutes). Garnish torte with whipped cream; serve with warm caramel sauce.

NUTRITION FACTS (1 SERVING)			
Calories	630	Fat	47g
Protein	4g	Cholesterol	100mg
Carbohydrate	56g	Sodium	102mg

ᴀᴘʀɪᴄᴏᴛ-ʟᴀᴄᴇᴅ ᴄʀᴇᴀᴍ ᴘᴜꜰꜰꜱ

PREPARATION TIME: 1 hour
BAKING TIME: 35 minutes COOLING TIME: 30 minutes

YIELD: 8 servings

CREAM PUFFS

1 cup water
½ cup LAND O LAKES® Butter
1 cup all-purpose flour
4 eggs

APRICOT CREAM

½ cup whipping cream, chilled
¼ cup powdered sugar
1 (8-ounce) package cream cheese, softened
½ teaspoon ground ginger
2 tablespoons apricot preserves

½ cup apricot preserves, melted
Powdered sugar

❖Heat oven to 400°. In 2-quart saucepan bring water and butter to a full boil. Stir in flour. Cook over low heat, stirring vigorously, until mixture forms a ball. Add eggs, one at a time, beating until smooth. Drop about ⅓ cup dough 3 inches apart onto cookie sheet. Bake for 35 to 40 minutes or until puffed and golden brown. Cool completely.

❖In chilled small mixer bowl beat whipping cream at high speed, scraping bowl often, until soft peaks form. Continue beating, gradually adding ¼ cup powdered sugar, until stiff peaks form (1 to 2 minutes). Add all remaining apricot cream ingredients except ½ cup apricot preserves and powdered sugar. Continue beating, scraping bowl often, until smooth (2 to 3 minutes).

❖Cut off cream puff tops; pull out any filaments of soft dough. Fill puffs with apricot cream; replace tops. Drizzle with melted apricot preserves; sprinkle with powdered sugar.

N U T R I T I O N F A C T S			
(1 Serving)			
Calories	430	Fat	30g
Protein	7g	Cholesterol	189mg
Carbohydrate	34g	Sodium	240mg

Pumpkin Squares

Preparation time: 30 minutes
Baking time: 50 minutes

Yield: 12 servings

CRUST
1 cup all-purpose flour
½ cup old-fashioned rolled oats
½ cup firmly packed brown sugar
½ cup Land O Lakes® Butter, softened

FILLING
¾ cup sugar
1 (15-ounce) can pumpkin
1 (12-ounce) can evaporated milk
2 eggs
1 teaspoon cinnamon
½ teaspoon salt
½ teaspoon ground ginger
¼ teaspoon ground cloves

TOPPING
½ cup firmly packed brown sugar
½ cup chopped pecans

GARNISH
Sweetened whipped cream, if desired

❖ Heat oven to 350°. In small mixer bowl combine all crust ingredients. Beat at low speed, scraping bowl often, until crumbly (1 to 2 minutes). Press on bottom of 13x9-inch baking pan. Bake for 15 minutes.

❖ Meanwhile, in large mixer bowl combine all filling ingredients. Beat at medium speed, scraping bowl often, until smooth (1 to 2 minutes); pour over crust. Continue baking 20 minutes.

❖ In small bowl stir together ½ cup brown sugar and pecans; sprinkle over filling. Continue baking for 15 to 25 minutes or until knife inserted in center comes out clean. Cool completely. Store refrigerated.

NUTRITION FACTS (1 SERVING)			
Calories	360	Fat	17g
Protein	6g	Cholesterol	75mg
Carbohydrate	49g	Sodium	220mg

$\mathcal{E}$asy $\mathcal{M}$ini-$\mathcal{C}$heesecakes

PREPARATION TIME: 30 minutes
BAKING TIME: 40 minutes CHILLING TIME: 1 hour

YIELD: 12 servings

CRUST
12 vanilla wafer
    cookies

FILLING
½ cup sugar
2 (8-ounce)
   packages cream
   cheese, softened
2 eggs
1 teaspoon vanilla
1 cup LAND O LAKES®
   Sour Cream
   (Regular, Light or
   No•Fat)
2 tablespoons
   sugar
1 teaspoon vanilla

GARNISH
   Chocolate curls, if
   desired
   Cut up fruit, if
   desired
   Powdered sugar,
   if desired

❖ Heat oven to 325°. Line 12-cup muffin pan with foil cupcake liners; place one cookie in each liner.

❖ In large mixer bowl combine ½ cup sugar, cream cheese, eggs and vanilla. Beat at medium speed, scraping bowl often, until creamy (2 to 3 minutes). Pour over each cookie, filling cup ¾ full. Bake for 30 minutes.

❖ Meanwhile, in small bowl stir together sour cream, 2 tablespoons sugar and vanilla. Spoon about 1 tablespoon sour cream mixture onto each hot cheesecake. Continue baking for 8 to 10 minutes or until set. Cool; remove from pan. Cover; refrigerate until firm (1 to 2 hours).

❖ To serve, garnish with chocolate curls, fruit and powdered sugar.

NUTRITION FACTS			
(1 SERVING)			
Calories	250	Fat	17g
Protein	5g	Cholesterol	85mg
Carbohydrate	20g	Sodium	150mg

Bavarian Apple Tart

PREPARATION TIME: 45 minutes
BAKING TIME: 40 minutes

YIELD: 12 servings

CRUST
1 cup all-purpose flour
⅓ cup sugar
½ cup LAND O LAKES® Butter, softened
¼ teaspoon vanilla

FILLING
½ cup sugar
2 (8-ounce) packages cream cheese, softened
2 eggs
1 teaspoon vanilla

4 medium (4 cups) tart cooking apples, peeled, sliced ¼ inch
⅓ cup sugar
½ teaspoon cinnamon
½ teaspoon ground nutmeg
Dash ground cardamom

¼ cup sliced almonds

GARNISH
Sweetened whipped cream

❖Heat oven to 375°. In small mixer bowl combine flour, ⅓ cup sugar, butter and ¼ teaspoon vanilla. Beat at medium speed, scraping bowl often, until dough leaves sides of bowl and forms a ball (2 to 3 minutes). With lightly floured hands, press on bottom of 10-inch springform pan.

❖In same small mixer bowl combine ½ cup sugar, cream cheese, eggs and 1 teaspoon vanilla. Beat at medium speed, scraping bowl often, until smooth (2 to 3 minutes). Spread over crust.

❖In large bowl place apples. Sprinkle with ⅓ cup sugar, cinnamon, nutmeg and cardamom; toss to coat. Arrange apples over filling.

❖Bake for 35 to 45 minutes or until apples are fork tender. Sprinkle with almonds; continue baking for 5 to 10 minutes or until almonds are lightly browned. Cool completely.

❖Remove rim from springform pan. Cut into wedges; serve with whipped cream.

Baked Lemon Pudding Souffle

PREPARATION TIME: 20 minutes
BAKING TIME: 45 minutes

YIELD: 6 servings

3 eggs, separated
1 cup sugar
⅓ cup LAND O LAKES® Butter, softened
¼ cup lemon juice
1 tablespoon grated lemon peel
¼ cup all-purpose flour
⅛ teaspoon salt
1 cup milk

Powdered sugar, if desired

❖Heat oven to 350°. In small mixer bowl beat egg whites at medium speed until foamy (1 to 2 minutes). Beat at high speed, gradually adding ¼ cup sugar, until stiff and glossy (2 to 3 minutes); set aside.

❖In large mixer bowl combine butter and remaining ¾ cup sugar. Beat at low speed, scraping bowl often, until creamy (1 to 2 minutes). Add egg yolks, lemon juice and peel; continue beating, scraping bowl often, until well mixed (1 minute). Add flour and salt; continue beating, scraping bowl often, until well mixed (1 minute). By hand, stir in milk. Fold beaten egg whites into butter mixture.

❖Pour mixture into 1½-quart casserole. Place casserole in 9-inch square baking pan. Place baking pan on oven rack; pour boiling water into baking pan to ½-inch depth. Bake for 45 to 55 minutes or until golden brown. Remove from water; cool 10 minutes. Sprinkle with powdered sugar.

COOL KEY LIME CHEESECAKE

PREPARATION TIME: 30 minutes
CHILLING TIME: 4 hours 45 minutes

YIELD: 12 servings

CRUST
1 cup graham cracker crumbs
¼ cup sugar
⅓ cup LAND O LAKES® Butter, melted

FILLING
1 cup lime juice
¼ cup water
2 (¼-ounce) envelopes unflavored gelatin
1½ cups sugar
5 eggs, slightly beaten
1 tablespoon grated lime peel
½ cup LAND O LAKES® Butter, softened
2 (8-ounce) packages cream cheese, softened
½ cup whipping cream

GARNISH
Sweetened whipped cream, if desired
Lime slices, if desired

❖ In medium bowl stir together all crust ingredients. Press on bottom of 9-inch springform pan; set aside.

❖ In 2-quart saucepan combine lime juice and water; sprinkle with gelatin. Let stand 5 minutes to soften. Add sugar, eggs and lime peel. Cook over medium heat, stirring constantly, until mixture just comes to a boil (7 to 8 minutes). DO NOT BOIL. Set aside.

❖ In large mixer bowl combine butter and cream cheese. Beat at medium speed, scraping bowl often, until well mixed (1 to 2 minutes). Continue beating, gradually adding hot lime mixture, until well mixed (1 to 2 minutes). Refrigerate, stirring occasionally, until cool (about 45 minutes).

❖ In chilled small mixer bowl beat chilled whipping cream at high speed, scraping bowl often, until stiff peaks form (1 to 2 minutes). Fold into lime mixture. Pour into prepared crust. Cover; refrigerate until firm (3 to 4 hours).

❖ Loosen sides of cheesecake from pan by running knife around inside of pan. Cool completely. Remove rim from springform pan. Garnish top of cheesecake with whipped cream and lime slices. Store refrigerated.

Apple Dumplings & Brandy Sauce

PREPARATION TIME: 1 hour
BAKING TIME: 35 minutes

YIELD: 6 servings (¾ cup)

DUMPLINGS

2   cups all-purpose flour
¼   teaspoon salt
½   cup LAND O LAKES® Butter, chilled
⅔   cup LAND O LAKES® Sour Cream (Regular, Light or No•Fat)
6   medium tart cooking apples, cored, peeled
⅓   cup sugar
⅓   cup chopped pecans
2   tablespoons LAND O LAKES® Butter, softened
    Milk

SAUCE

½   cup firmly packed brown sugar
2   tablespoons LAND O LAKES® Butter
½   cup whipping cream
1   tablespoon brandy*

* Substitute 1 teaspoon brandy extract.

✦Heat oven to 400°. In medium bowl stir together flour and salt; cut in ½ cup butter until mixture forms coarse crumbs. With fork, stir in sour cream until mixture leaves sides of bowl and forms a ball.

✦On lightly floured surface roll dough into 19x12-inch rectangle. Cut 1-inch strip off 19-inch end; reserve. Cut remaining dough into 6 (6-inch) squares. Place apple in center of each square.

✦In small bowl stir together sugar, pecans and 2 tablespoons butter. Stuff 1½ tablespoons into cored center of each apple. Fold dough up around apple; seal seams well. Place seam side down on greased 15x10x1-inch jelly roll pan.

✦Brush dough with milk; prick dough with fork. Cut leaf designs out of reserved 1-inch strip of dough. Brush with milk; place on wrapped apples. Bake for 35 to 50 minutes or until apples are fork tender. If crust browns too quickly, cover with aluminum foil.

✦In 1-quart saucepan combine all sauce ingredients. Cook over medium heat, stirring occasionally, until mixture comes to a full boil (3 to 4 minutes). Serve sauce over warm dumplings.

NUTRITION FACTS (1 SERVING)			
Calories	690	Fat	37g
Protein	7g	Cholesterol	96mg
Carbohydrate	87g	Sodium	360mg

STRAWBERRY-RHUBARB COBBLER

PREPARATION TIME: 30 minutes
COOLING TIME: 1 hour BAKING TIME: 55 minutes

YIELD: 16 servings

FILLING
1   (16-ounce) package
    frozen sliced strawberries,
    thawed
1   pound (4 cups) rhubarb,
    cut into 1-inch pieces*
2   tablespoons lemon juice
1   cup sugar
⅓   cup cornstarch

CAKE
3   cups all-purpose flour
1   cup sugar
1   teaspoon baking powder
1   teaspoon baking soda
1   teaspoon salt
1   cup LAND O LAKES® Butter,
    chilled
1   cup LAND O LAKES® Sour
    Cream (Regular, Light or
    No•Fat)
2   eggs
3   tablespoons milk
1   teaspoon vanilla

TOPPING
⅓   cup sugar
½   cup sliced almonds

    Half-and-half or ice cream,
    if desired

*   Substitute 1 (16-ounce)
    package frozen sliced
    rhubarb, thawed.

❖ In 3-quart saucepan combine strawberries and rhubarb. Cook over medium heat until mixture comes to a full boil (10 to 15 minutes). Reduce heat to low. Cover; cook 5 minutes. Stir in lemon juice.

❖ In small bowl combine 1 cup sugar and cornstarch. Stir into fruit mixture. Cook over medium heat, stirring occasionally, until mixture thickens and just comes to a boil. Boil 1 minute; cool.

❖ Heat oven to 350°. In large bowl combine flour, 1 cup sugar, baking powder, baking soda and salt; cut in butter until crumbly.

❖ In medium bowl combine all remaining cake ingredients; beat with wire whisk until smooth. Stir sour cream mixture into flour mixture just until moistened. Spread half of batter on bottom of greased 13x9-inch baking pan. Spread with cooled fruit mixture. Drop remaining batter by spoonfuls over fruit filling.

❖ Sprinkle batter with ⅓ cup sugar and sliced almonds. Bake for 55 to 70 minutes or until toothpick inserted in center comes out clean. Serve warm or cool with half-and-half or ice cream.

TIP
Use a 13x9-inch aluminum baking pan that is at least 2½ inches deep; do not use a 13x9-inch glass pan.

TEA BISCUITS WITH BLUSHING RASPBERRIES

PREPARATION TIME: 25 minutes   BAKING TIME: 10 minutes

YIELD: 8 servings

BISCUITS
2 cups all-purpose flour
½ cup sugar
1 tablespoon baking powder
½ teaspoon salt
⅔ cup LAND O LAKES® Butter, chilled
½ cup whipping cream
2 tablespoons orange juice

WHIPPED CREAM
1 cup whipping cream
2 tablespoons sugar
1 teaspoon vanilla

RASPBERRY SAUCE
1 pint fresh raspberries*
⅓ cup powdered sugar
¼ cup orange juice

1 pint fresh raspberries

*Substitute 1 (10-ounce) package frozen raspberries.

❖ Heat oven to 400°. In large bowl combine flour, ½ cup sugar, baking powder and salt; cut in butter until crumbly. Stir in ½ cup whipping cream and 2 tablespoons orange juice just until moistened.

❖ Turn dough onto lightly floured surface; knead until smooth (1 minute). Roll out to ½-inch thickness. With 2-inch scalloped round or heart-shaped cutter, cut out 8 biscuits. Place 1 inch apart on cookie sheet. Bake for 10 to 14 minutes or until lightly browned.

❖ Meanwhile, in chilled small mixer bowl beat 1 cup chilled whipping cream at high speed, scraping bowl often, until soft peaks form. Continue beating, gradually adding 2 tablespoons sugar, until stiff peaks form (1 to 2 minutes). By hand, gently stir in vanilla.

❖ In 5-cup blender container place 1 pint raspberries, powdered sugar and ¼ cup orange juice. Blend on high speed until pureed (1 to 2 minutes). If desired, strain sauce to remove seeds. Place biscuits in individual dessert dishes. Serve with raspberry sauce, whipped cream and fresh raspberries.

WARM PEAR CRISP

PREPARATION TIME: 20 minutes
BAKING TIME: 40 minutes

YIELD: 6 servings

FILLING
4 medium (4 cups) pears, peeled, sliced ½ inch
1 tablespoon lemon juice
1 teaspoon cinnamon
½ teaspoon ground nutmeg

TOPPING
½ cup all-purpose flour
½ cup quick-cooking oats
½ cup firmly packed brown sugar
⅓ cup LAND O LAKES® Butter, softened

Ice cream or sweetened whipped cream, if desired

❖ Heat oven to 375°. Place pears in 9-inch square baking pan. Sprinkle with lemon juice, cinnamon and nutmeg.

❖ In small mixer bowl combine flour, oats, brown sugar and butter. Beat at low speed, scraping bowl often, until crumbly (1 to 2 minutes). Sprinkle evenly over pears.

❖ Bake for 40 to 50 minutes or until pears are fork tender and top is golden brown. Serve warm with ice cream or whipped cream.

BAVARIAN CUSTARD

PREPARATION TIME: 10 minutes
CHILLING TIME: 2 hours

YIELD: 6 servings

1 (3.4-ounce) package instant vanilla flavor pudding and pie filling*
1 cup milk
1 cup LAND O LAKES® Sour Cream (Regular, Light or No•Fat)
1 (8-ounce) carton (1 cup) low-fat vanilla flavored yogurt

Fresh strawberries, raspberries, blueberries or blackberries**

* Substitute 1 (0.9-ounce) package sugar-free instant vanilla pudding and pie filling

** Substitute frozen thawed berries.

❖ In medium bowl place instant pudding. With wire whisk, stir in milk until mixture is smooth and slightly thickened.

❖ Add sour cream and yogurt; whisk until smooth. Cover; refrigerate at least 2 hours.

❖ Spoon custard into 6 individual dessert dishes; top with assorted berries.

NUTRITION FACTS (1 SERVING)			
Calories	160	Fat	3g
Protein	5g	Cholesterol	10mg
Carbohydrate	29g	Sodium	320mg

Raspberry Crowned Chocolate Torte

Preparation time: 1 hour Baking time: 40 minutes
Cooling time: 1 hour Chilling time: 2 hours

Yield: 12 servings

3 eggs, separated
⅛ teaspoon cream of tartar
⅛ teaspoon salt
1½ cups sugar
1 cup Land O Lakes® Butter, melted
1½ teaspoons vanilla
½ cup all-purpose flour
½ cup unsweetened cocoa
3 tablespoons water
¾ cup finely chopped almonds

⅓ cup raspberry preserves

Sweetened whipped cream, if desired
Fresh raspberries, if desired

❖ Heat oven to 350°. Grease 9-inch round cake pan. Line with aluminum foil, leaving excess foil over edges; grease foil. Set aside.

❖ In small mixer bowl combine egg whites, cream of tartar and salt. Beat at high speed, scraping bowl often, until soft peaks form (1 to 2 minutes); set aside.

❖ In large mixer bowl combine egg yolks, sugar, butter and vanilla. Beat at medium speed, scaping bowl often, until well mixed (1 to 2 minutes). Add flour, cocoa and water. Continue beating, scraping bowl often, until well mixed (1 to 2 minutes). Stir in chopped almonds. Fold beaten egg whites into chocolate mixture.

❖ Spread into prepared pan. Bake for 40 to 55 minutes or until firm to the touch. DO NOT OVERBAKE. Cool on wire rack 1 hour; remove from pan by lifting aluminum foil.

❖ Cover; refrigerate until completely cooled (2 to 3 hours). Remove aluminum foil; place on serving plate. Spread raspberry preserves on top. Garnish with sweetened whipped cream and raspberries.

NUTRITION FACTS (1 Serving)			
Calories	350	Fat	22g
Protein	5g	Cholesterol	110mg
Carbohydrate	38g	Sodium	225mg

Layered Pralines & Cream

PREPARATION TIME: 30 minutes BAKING TIME: 16 minutes
COOKING TIME: 8 minutes CHILLING TIME: 1 hour

YIELD: 6 servings

CRUNCH MIXTURE
¼ cup LAND O LAKES® Butter
½ cup bite-size crispy rice cereal squares
½ cup flaked coconut
½ cup slivered almonds
½ cup firmly packed brown sugar
½ cup chopped pecans

CUSTARD
½ cup sugar
1 cup milk
1 egg, slightly beaten
1 tablespoon cornstarch
1 teaspoon vanilla
1 cup whipping cream, whipped

❖ Heat oven to 325°. In 15x10x1-inch jelly roll pan melt butter in oven (4 to 5 minutes). Add remaining crunch mixture ingredients; stir to coat well. Bake for 12 to 14 minutes, stirring occasionally, until golden brown. Cool completely; crumble cereal.

❖ Meanwhile, in 2-quart saucepan combine all custard ingredients <u>except</u> vanilla and whipped cream. Cook over medium heat, stirring often, until mixture comes to a full boil (7 to 9 minutes). Boil 1 minute. Remove from heat; stir in vanilla. Cover surface with plastic food wrap; refrigerate until cooled completely (1 to 2 hours).

❖ Fold whipped cream into custard mixture. Just before serving, alternate layers of custard and crunch mixture in dessert glasses.

Index

Save 17% when you receive 6 issues, each filled with irresistible recipes, delivered right to your door.

Now you can subscribe to the LAND O LAKES® Recipe Collection™ and get delicious recipes right in your mailbox! Pay only $14.95 for 6 exciting issues and save from the magazine-rack price. Or order 12 issues and pay just $23.95.

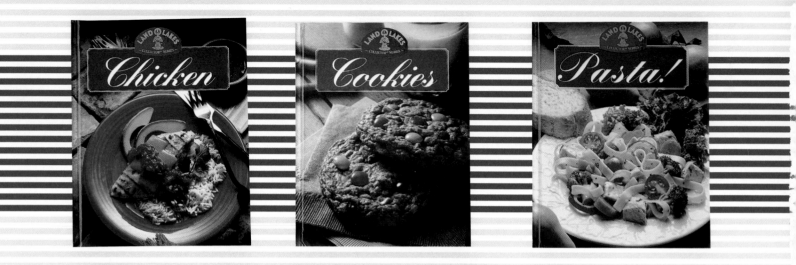